A CONCISE HISTORY OF THE UNITED STATES

WITH DOCUMENTS

LEWIS HOUSE
JON E. PURMONT
IRA LEONARD
Southern Connecticut State University

,

TLI Press

New Haven   New York

TABLE OF CONTENTS

I	The Discovery of the New World	1
II	The Colonial Experience, 1607-1763	6
III	The American Revolution, 1776-1783	10
IV	Constitution and the New Republic, 1781-1800p	14
V	The Era of Thomas Jefferson, 1801-1824	19
VI	The Era of Andrew Jackson, 1828-1848	24
VII	Economic Change, Westward Expansion and Sectional Discord, 1820-1860	28
VIII	The Coming of War, 1848-1860	33
IX	The Civil War and Reconstruction, 1861-1877	37
X	Industrial Expansion, 1876-1900	42
XI	The Progressive Era, 1900-1920	46
XII	From World War to Economic Depression, 1917-1929	51
XIII	Depression and the New Deal, 1929-1940	55
XIV	World War II, 1941-1945	60
XV	Harry Truman and the Beginning of the Cold War, 1945-1953	64
XVI	The Eisenhower Administration, 1953-1961	69
XVII	John F. Kennedy-Lyndon Johnson, 1961-1969	73
XVIII	Richard M. Nixon, 1969-1977	80
XIX	Jimmy Carter, 1977-1981	85
XX	The Era of Ronald Reagan, 1981-1989	89
XXI	George Bush, 1989-1993	94
XXII	The Clinton Years, 1993-	99

Documents

A Letter of Christopher Columbus	104
Mayflower Compact	106
William Bradford of Plymouth Plantation	107
Fundamental Orders of Connecticut	109
Selections From Connecticut's Early Laws	110
Resolutions of the Stamp Act Congress	113
Benjamin Franklin Responds to House of Commons	114
Declaration of Independence	120
Articles of Confederation	124
The Northwest Ordinance	126
Constitution of the United States	128
Report on Manufactures by Alexander Hamilton	148
Alien and Sedition Acts	150
Marbury v. Madison	152
Constitution of Connecticut	154
Missouri Crisis and Impact	157
James Monroe, Message to Congress	159
Andrew Jackson Endorses Indian Removal	160
Andrew Jackson Vetoes the Bank	161

Seneca Falls Declaration   162
Dred Scott v. Sandford   166
Slavery in the South   169
Lincoln-Douglas Debate   170
State of Mississippi-Orders of Secession   173
The Gettysburg Address   175
Abraham Lincoln's Second Inaugural Address   176
Black Codes of Louisiana   177
The South Must be Punished   179
Civil Rights Act of 1875   180
Chinese Exclusion Act   181
Excerpts from Cheap Labor   181
Populist Party Platform   183
Plessy v. Ferguson   185
William McKinley's War Message   188
Roosevelt Corollary to the Monroe Doctrine   190
Woodrow Wilson's New Freedom   191
Woodrow Wilson on Neutrality   193
Herbert Hoover on American Values   194
Franklin D. Roosevelt Inaugural Address   196
Franklin D. Roosevelt's "Four Freedoms" Speech   201
Franklin D. Roosevelt War Message-Japan   203
The Truman Doctrine   205
Truman's Statement on Korea   209
Internal Security Act   210
Senator Margaret Chase Smith Speaks Out Against McCarthyism   212
Brown v. Board of Education   214
Eisenhower Sends Federal Troops   215
Dwight D. Eisenhower's Farewell Address   217
John F. Kennedy Inaugural Address   219
John F. Kennedy and the Cuban Missile Crisis   221
John F. Kennedy and the Strategy of Peace   223
Gulf of Tonkin Resolution   229
Lyndon B. Johnson and the Great Society   230
President Johnson Supports Civil Rights   232
President Johnson Asserts His War Aims   234
The Kerner Report   235
Richard Nixon Sends Troops to Cambodia   237
White House Conversations   239
George Bush on Aggression in the Gulf   243
President Bill Clinton's Remarks   245

Attributions

Chapter I -- The Discovery of the New World

Time Line

1096-1291   European Crusades to the Holy Land
1492   Christopher Columbus makes first voyage to America
1498   Vasco da Gama sailed to India
1522   Hernan Cortes conquered Mexico
1533   Francisco Pizarro reached Peru
1607   First Permanent English settlement in Jamestown, Virginia

Key Terms

Crusades
Commercial companies
Alternative routes
Landed gentry
Indios

Background

The discovery of the New World (consisting of North and South America and the Caribbean Islands) was the result of a great wave of European exploration and colonization beginning in the 1400's.

Rivalries erupted between emerging nation-states (Portugal, Spain, England, France and the Netherlands) between 1000 and 1500 over lands in Europe, over religious conflicts (between Catholics and Protestants in Europe, and the Crusades between Christians and Muslims in the Near East), trade, overseas possessions, and raw materials. These rivalries led, among other things, to the opening of new trade routes, the application of new technology to shipbuilding and weaponry (cannons placed on ships) and new navigation tools (new maps, magnetic compass and marine charts), all of which acted to accelerate Europeans' overseas activities.

Prince Henry the Navigator

In the late 1300's Prince Henry founded a school for navigators in Lisbon, Portugal that drew experienced seamen from all over Europe. Starting in 1415, the Portuguese took control of a base in North Africa and began to explore the Atlantic coast of Africa. By the 1450's they had a line of

1

fortified trading posts along the coast and a thriving trade with native African chiefs for various commodities (ebony wood, ivory, animal skins) and Black African slaves. The slaves were taken to Portugal and to their colonies on the Canary and Madeira islands off the African coast and Azores far out in the Atlantic Ocean. They had proven by the mid-1400's that they could use the ocean like a highway and become rich and powerful from these trade routes. In 1498 Vasco da Gama made the first trip around the tip of Africa out to India, opening yet another new and profitable trade network and began a new wave of European overseas expansion. At the same time, in 1500, a ship captain Pedro Cabral, blown off course, landed on the northern most tip of Brazil, in South America, and claimed it for Portugal.

The Discovery of the Americas

Probably the first Europeans to discover the Americas were the Norse seamen around the year 1000. But their voyages to Nova Scotia and Maine were not followed up with permanent settlements and were forgotten in Norway over time, and no one in Europe learned of these voyages.

Christopher Columbus, a Genoese ship captain, had a plan to sail across the Atlantic Ocean to Japan as early as 1460, but was rejected by the Portuguese and delayed by the Spanish. Finally, in September 1492, the Spanish monarchs agreed to the plan and gave him three ships for the expedition. Sailing from the port of Palos, Spain, Columbus landed in the Bahamas, in the West Indies some 33 days later. Although Columbus made a total of four trips to the Caribbean and established the first permanent Spanish colonies on the islands of San Salvador and Cuba, he died in the belief that he had actually found the outlying islands of Asia.

The New World Peoples

The New World peoples called "Indios" by Columbus had migrated from Asia some 10,000 to 20,000 years before the birth of Christ when Siberia and Alaska had been joined. Over thousands of years, they spread over North and South America, and out onto the Caribbean Islands, forming a wide variety of different living patterns as they adapted to different geographical and climactic conditions. By the time of Columbus's 1492 voyage, there were more than 200 different Indian languages and dialects spoken in South America alone. Of all the Indian communities in the Americas, the largest and most complex were the Aztecs in Mexico, Mayas in Central America, and Incas in Peru.

2

The Spanish in America

The aims of the Spanish monarchs were to glorify God, become rich and powerful from overseas trade and possessions, and open a new glorious page in Spanish history. At first they were disappointed with what Columbus brought back to Spain (some birds, trinkets, and a few native Indians), but no gold, silver, precious stones or spices. All of this changed in 1522 when Hernan Cortes, who sailed westward from Cuba, took control of the Aztec empire centered in Mexico. The silver and gold of the Aztecs amazed the Spanish and the search for mineral wealth all but consumed the Spanish from that point. They received permission to explore the areas of North America but found no large Indian settlements, nor vast mineral resources and returned to Mexico and the Caribbean. But in 1533 they were rewarded when Francisco Pizarro, exploring southward into South America, landed in Peru and conquered the Incan empire that was rich in gold and silver.

Both Cortes and Pizarro, like earlier Spanish conquerors in the Caribbean, prevailed over numerically superior Indian communities because the Indians died of disease (like measles and small pox, for which they had no immunity) and Spanish weaponry and aggressiveness. To compensate for the loss of Indian workers on the West Indian islands, the Spanish had imported Black African slaves (slavery: life servitude passed on to one's children) from the Portuguese traders, starting in 1501. Although Indians on the mainland died by the hundreds of thousands, there were other Indians to take their places in the mines and on the landed estates of the Spanish.

The Spanish New World Empire

The Spanish created the largest European-based empire since the Romans, a thousand years earlier. Ruling through a small number of advisors, two large government agencies (the Council of the Indies and Casa de Contraction) and the Catholic Church, and an army of royal appointees, the Spanish monarchs were able to maintain royal authority over their New World possessions and peoples (mainly conquered native Indians) until 1825. Thus for close to 400 years Spain drew upon the wealth of the New World colonies to finance its activities and in return provided the New World peoples with Christianity, Spanish language and culture.

Beginnings of Colonization in North America

Based on voyages by their own naval personnel, England and France both laid claim to considerable portions of North America, north of the Spanish colonies, during the late 1500's and early 1600's. The monarchs made grants to commercial companies or groups of individuals to settle different areas at that time. These companies not only settled the land but had the right to govern it.

Small countries like the Netherlands and Sweden had interests in North America but they did not have the necessary resources for permanent colonization. The English began serious colonization efforts in the 1580's with the expeditions of Humphrey Gilbert and then Walter Raleigh. The first permanent English settlement came in 1607 when 104 people founded Jamestown, Virginia for a commercial company based in London. It was not an immediate success. However, the production of tobacco to be exported to England provided an economic base for survival. By 1618, 50,000 pounds of tobacco was sent to England and the British were engaged in the planning of new colonies.

Chapter I -- The Discovery of the New World
Review Questions

_____ 1. The Navigation school run by Prince Henry in Portugal had seamen study all except A) Improved map making B) Better navigational techniques C) Training sailors D) Language training in Indian dialects.

_____ 2. Christopher Columbus was considered a failure by the Spanish because he did not A) Actually land in Asia B) Bring back mineral wealth to Spain C) Took too long to reach America D) Discover Brazil.

_____ 3. The first English colony in the New World was A) Charlestown B) Boston C) Jamestown D) Delaware.

_____ 4 The primary export from Virginia to England was A) Rice B) Furs C) Tobacco D) Tea.

_____ 5. Spain explored the Atlantic coast north to Cape Cod but did not stay because A) Indians were too hostile B) No evidence of mineral wealth C) The soil was not fertile enough to plant crops D) Not enough settlers were available for colonization.

_____ 6. This European country had early settlements in North America but not the resources to stay A) Finland B) Germany C) Monaco D) The Netherlands.

_____ 7. Vasco da Gama made a successful trip around Africa in 1498 and landed in A) Asia B) Japan C) India D) China.

_____ 8. Two of the major Indian civilizations in the New World were A) Maya and Zulu B) Norse and Inca C) Arawak and Zuni D) Inca and Maya.

_____ 9. The main reason for European exploration in the 15th and 16th centuries was A) Colonization for slavery B) Spread the gospel C) Find new water routes to Africa D) Bring back wealth to Europe

_____ 10. Holy wars beginning in the 11th century were called A) Crusades B) Revolutions C) Hundred Years War D) Civil Wars

Time Line

1607   Jamestown, Virginia colony established
1620   Plymouth, Massachusetts colony founded
1660   Navigation acts passed

Key Terms

Self governing colony
Colonial Assemblies
Uni-Cameral Legislature
Mercantilism

Background

While England began its colonization of the New World after Spain, it was able to achieve more success than any other European country. The northern part of America seemed less attractive to colonize. There were no advanced civilizations to take advantage of or great amounts of mineral resources to extract from the ground. In the long run the absence of quick riches and the desire of the English settlers to work the land laid the foundation upon which an independent country could be built.

Problems of Colonization

Although the climate of North America's Atlantic region was similar to that of Western Europe, there were some problems that made settlement difficult. The winters were longer and colder than Europe and in the south summers were hotter and much more humid. Travel was difficult because of the complete lack of roads. Expansion westward moved along the various waterways which ran from the mountains in the west down to the Atlantic coast.

Before the end of the 1600's, the English had firmly established a strong presence in North America. Their settlements ran from Maine in the north to South Carolina in the south, a distance of more than 1000 miles. These colonies were divided into three geographical areas -- the New England colonies (Massachusetts, Rhode Island, Connecticut, Vermont and New Hampshire), the Middle Colonies (New York, New Jersey, Pennsylvania) and

Southern Colonies (Delaware, Maryland, Virginia, North and South Carolina, and after 1732, Georgia).

Population and Immigration

Economic improvement (primarily in the form of land ownership) was the chief factor motivating European settlers to migrate to the British North American colonies in the 1600's and 1700's. Other reasons for coming included the desire to practice religion free from restrictions. Those who came for religious reasons included the Puritans (who settled the New England colonies), a variety of other Protestant denominations, Catholics, and a scattering of Jews from various areas of Europe.

Fifty to seventy five percent of those who migrated to the colonies between 1650 and 1750 were too poor to pay their passage way and signed work contracts (called indentured servant contracts) requiring them to work from 4 to 7 years.

Another significant group of immigrants were Black Africans who were brought in as slaves, beginning in 1619 (in Virginia). By the Revolution slaves were to be found in all 13 colonies but mainly concentrated in the Southern colonies working on large landed estates growing cash crops (tobacco, rice, and indigo).

The population of the colonies reached an estimated 1.5 million people by 1763.

British Imperialism

The empire was run on the theory of mercantilism. Therefore the purpose of having a colony was to make a profit for the mother country. Raw materials were traditionally taken from the colony and shipped to the mother country where they could be turned into finished products and re-sold to the settlers at a higher price. This policy was administered by the British in America through a series of legislative acts known as the Trade and Navigation Acts.

The British, however, only enforced these regulations from time to time. Colonists became used to avoiding the Navigation Acts and as a result their profits grew. When, in the mid-18th, the English attempted vigorously to enforce these laws they were met with a firestorm of protest.

Political Growth of Colonial America

In political matters nearly every colony had become virtually self-governing. While there were appointed royal officials in each colony, the very distance between England and America made strict enforcement of regulations difficult.

Each colony had its own legislature, usually uni-cameral. It was elected by white male property owners. During the colonial period there was a gradual shift of power from the royal governors to the colonial legislatures.

Political power was held by colonial landowners and exercised through town or county governments and the colonial assemblies. Voting was legally restricted in all of the colonies to white, male landowners and in some colonies to members of a particular church. Women, African-Americans and Indians had no political rights in the 13 colonies.

Growth of Democracy

As settlers prospered and grew in numbers they began to think of themselves as Americans not English citizens. The traditional basis for class society in England was built on land ownership. This became obsolete in America with more than enough land available. Class distinctions seemed to blur. People seemed more alike than different. Benjamin Franklin stated, "It is rather a genial mediocrity that prevails."

Chapter II -- The Colonial Experience, 1607-1763
Review Questions

_____ 1. Most English settlers worked in A) Manufacturing B) Agriculture C) Home Trades D) Fishing

_____ 2 England operated its colonial empire on the theory of A) Mercantilism B) Empiricism C) Laissez Faire D) Transcendentalism

_____ 3. Essentially the mother country made a profit from colonies by extracting from them A) Water B) Finished Products C) Technology D) Raw Materials

_____ 4. Trade and Navigation Acts were set up to A) Provoke the colonists B) Regulate trade to and from the colonies C) Regulate merchant marine D) Did not apply to America

_____ 5. The traditional basis for wealth in Europe was A) Land B) Gold C) Children D) Cattle

_____ 6. Self-governance in the colonies took place because A) Liberality of English law B) Growth of democracy in the colonies C) Distance from England D) Newspaper editorials

_____ 7. Colonial legislatures usually took the following form A) English B) Uni-Cameral C) An appointed lower house D) An elected upper house

_____ 8. The colonies were populated by people seeking A) Religious freedom B) Mineral wealth C) Men seeking wives D) Increased economic trade

_____ 9. It was estimated that the population of the American colonies in 1763 was A) 500,000 B) 50,000 C) 1,500,000 D) 5,000,000

_____ 10. Voting rights were restricted to A) White, male landowners B) Men and women over the age of 21 C) All males over the age of 21 D) All free men

Chapter III -- The American Revolution, 1776-1783

Time Line

1763   End of the French and Indian War
1764   British Taxation Policy Begins - Sugar Act
1765   Stamp Act
1773   Boston Tea Party
1776   Declaration of Independence
1783   Treaty of Paris - End of the American Revolution

Key Terms

Continental Congress
Human Rights
Authoritarian Government
Hereditary Rights
Consent of the Governed

Background

The very distance between Colonial America and England made a certain amount of independence necessary. American self-reliance did not aim to repudiate British rule but to gain for the colonies equal status under British law. After the French and Indian War (1756-1763), Britain initiated an imperial policy designed to recover its costs for fighting the war and, in addition, to regulate and control the colonies. These policies angered the Americans and spurred the independence movement.

Colonial Objectives

There were complex motives for joining the independence movement. Not all Americans wanted British rule ended. Growing numbers of merchants and planters wanted to be rid of the restrictive colonial laws that hindered economic growth. There were still others who demanded greater political rights. They wanted to end what they considered a system that created aristocratic privilege in the colonies.

British Colonial Policy 1763-1776

The lack of effective leadership in England only made matters worse. Parliament's tax program placed duties on sugar (1764) and stamps (1765) and ignited widespread defiance among the colonists. A boycott of English products was so successful that the taxes were repealed in 1766. Instead of building a new relationship with the colonies, a new government in England imposed more taxes. These became known as the Townshend Acts (1767). Later, a tax on tea was introduced and this led directly to the Boston Tea Party (1773) when two million pounds of tea were dumped into Boston Harbor by American patriots.

The British retaliated by enacting legislation that so angered the colonists that they termed them the "Intolerable Acts". This legislation made it clear to the Americans that they had no political rights under English law.

Declaration of Independence

The war broke out in April 1775 at Lexington and Concord. The colonies then created the Continental Congress in September 1775.

In the Spring of 1776 the Congress advised the colonies to establish independent governments. Between 1776 and 1784 each colony transformed itself into a separate state by drafting its own constitution. Following Virginia's example, all the new state constitutions included a bill of rights defining citizenship rights, such as freedom of religion, speech, press and assembly.

A committee of the Continental Congress, headed by Thomas Jefferson, was appointed on July 2, 1776 to draw up a resolution of independence and on July 4, 1776 Congress accepted the Declaration of Independence.

Jefferson's task had been to give expression to the political sentiments held by most Americans. The result was a document that was an affirmation of human rights. The United States had turned its back on hereditary rights and authoritarian government. All men were considered equal and government was to derive its power from the "consent of the governed."

War 1775-1783

While the British troops were better paid, equipped and fed, the colonists had certain advantages. The Americans knew the terrain and tended to be excellent shots. George Washington was appointed General of the Continental Army. While not a military tactician, he had strong personality and was able to lead his army in the field for eight years.

The biggest obstacle to an American victory seemed to be the danger that the inexperienced colonials might lose the will to fight and their army might melt away. The British won most of the early battles, but were unable to hold on to much of the territory. As the war progressed, the colonists received significant aid from Spain and France.

On October 19, 1781 British General Cornwallis was compelled to surrender at Yorktown. The British decided that it was useless to continue fighting and there was little further action.

Peace Treaty

The Treaty of Paris was signed in 1783. England conceded that the American colonies were now independent. The British also gave up all claims to territory located south of the Great Lakes and east of the Mississippi River.

Results of the Revolution

Independence was secured with the signing of the Treaty of Paris (1783). Among the results of the Revolution were that slavery was gradually phased out in all of the states north of Delaware. Middle class citizens now had the opportunity, in greater numbers, to enter politics and become elected officials.

Chapter III -- The American Revolution, 1776-1783
Review Questions

_____ 1. Colonists were angry at England after 1763 because of A) English trade restrictions; B) Erratic English officials; C) Abandonment of the colonies by the British; D) British Taxation policies.

_____ 2. The English decision to raise colonial taxes came as a result of A) War of the Roses; B) French and Indian War; C) English greed; D) Economic recession in England

_____ 3. The acts that led to the American Revolution were called A) Intolerable Acts; B) Alien and Sedition Acts; C) Trade and Navigation Acts; D) Royal fiat

_____ 4. The Declaration of Independence was basically considered to be the work of A) Thomas Jefferson; B) George Washington; C) Thomas Paine; D) Benjamin Franklin

_____ 5. The Boston Tea Party came as a direct result of the A) Stamp Act; B) Tea Act; C) Sugar Act; D) Grain Act

_____ 6. The head of the Continental Army was A) George Washington; B) Thomas Jefferson; C) James Madison; D) Lord Cornwallis

_____ 7. The treaty to end the American Revolution was signed in A) London; B) Washington; C) Paris; D) Rome

_____ 8. The Declaration of Independence stated that government was to get its powers from A) Elected officials; B) Consent of the governed; C) Appointed officials; D) Governors

_____ 9. The British surrender at this battle was the turning point of the Revolution A) Long Island; B) Hartford; C) Trenton; D) Yorktown

_____ 10. Americans reacted to English tax laws by A) Organizing boycotts; B) Aiding the French; C) Impressing sailors; D) Withdrawing from trade

Chapter IV -- Constitution and the New Republic, 1781-1800

Time Line

1781   Articles of Confederation adopted
1787   Connecticut Compromise set up Houses of Congress
1789   Constitutional government adopted
         George Washington sworn in as President
1796   John Adams became President
1797   XYZ Affair with France
1798   Alien and Sedition Acts
         Virginia and Kentucky Resolutions

Key Terms

Confederation
Federalists
Anti-Federalists
Sedition Act
Alien Act
Legislative, Judicial, Executive branches of government
Hamilton's Four Reports

Political Background

During the American Revolution there were lively discussions about what form of government the new nation should adopt. Those who wanted a strong central government were known as 'Federalists'. The other group favored a weak central government and were called the 'Anti-Federalists'. Political struggles between these two groups defined the 1780's and early 1790's.

Articles of Confederation

The first national government was called the Articles of Confederation, adopted in 1781. It was a victory for those who favored a weak central government with the power vested in the 13 state governments. The national government was a Congress or single legislative body composed of representatives sent from the states; it did not have the power to levy taxes, raise an army or coin money, which were considered essential to the authority of a national government. Thus the confederation was more like an association of states where the power rested with local authorities. By the mid-1780's, there was a growing feeling among influential Americans, like George Washington and Thomas Jefferson, that the national government had to be able to exercise national powers independent of the states. Finally,

14

in 1787, Congress was persuaded to call for a constitutional convention to draft amendments to the Articles.

United States Constitution of 1787

Most of the 55 delegates who met in Philadelphia between May and September 1787 wanted to create a government strong enough to protect the nation, pay its debts, establish an effective foreign policy, and promote economic growth and development while at the same time protecting individual liberty.

The framers of the new document agreed that the new government should consist of three branches, with a separate Legislative, Executive, and Judiciary, modeled to some extent on the system of old colonial and new state governments. Each branch would be independent of the others but the Constitution required them to cooperate and also to "check and balance" the others, all in the interest of protecting the liberty of American citizens.

Two Difficult Problems

The two most difficult problems facing the delegates were how to arrange representation in the national legislative body (called the Congress) and how to handle the issue of human slavery. A compromise (called the Connecticut or Great Compromise) established a two house Congress. The House of Representatives was to be set up on the basis of state population which pleased the large states while the Senate would have equal representation with two votes which pleased the small states. At the urging of delegates from the southern states where slavery still existed, a compromise was arranged, including the counting of five slaves as three whites for representation purposes in the House of Representatives (the 'three fifths' clause), fugitive slaves were to be returned, and the importation of slaves was not to be prohibited until 1808. Slavery was protected but not guaranteed in the Constitution. This compromise would become a source of increasing friction between northern and southern states.

Foreign Policy

Foreign policy and national defense was put jointly into the hands of the national executive (called the President) and Congress. The President was limited to a four year term but could be reelected any number of times (this was changed to two terms or 10 years in the 22nd amendment, 1951) and an indirect system of presidential election (the electoral college) was put into effect.

Although there was a narrow majority of support for the new Constitution, there was fear that such a strong central government could threaten individual liberty. Therefore, five of the state conventions ratified the Constitution on the condition that a national Bill of Rights, like those in each of the state constitutions, be added.

Bill of Rights

In 1791, ten amendments that guaranteed individual liberties were added to the Constitution. They included the rights of freedom of speech, religion and press, and a series of protections for citizens who were accused of a crime, such as trial by jury, right of counsel, and the guarantee that no person could be deprived of life, liberty or property without due process of law. Women received no legal protections in either the Constitution or the Bill of Rights.

The Washington Administration 1789-1797

George Washington was the unanimous choice of the electoral college and he became the first President of the United States. The main task of his administration was to establish the new government and put the country on a sound economic footing. Secretary of the Treasury Alexander Hamilton drew up a series of proposals that recommended the national government pay off the national and states debts (about 77 million dollars) from the Revolutionary War, institute a variety of taxes, a schedule of western land sales, a protective tariff on imported goods, a national bank to facilitate these arrangements and plans to have the government encourage manufacturing in America. Passage of most of these proposals led to the emergence of the first political parties in the nation. Those who supported the administration called themselves the 'Federalists' while those following the opposition leader, Thomas Jefferson, used the name 'Democratic-Republicans'. Political divisions also developed over the administration foreign policy. What should the U.S. position toward France be after the French Revolution erupted in 1789? Secondly, how to rebuild American relations with England and Spain.

John Adams 1797-1801

John Adams, Vice President under George Washington, won a close vote in the electoral college when he defeated Thomas Jefferson, 71-68 in 1796. Thus Adams became the President and his opponent became Vice President.

Foreign policy problems continued to haunt the nation. The French were angered over the apparent reconciliation between the United States and England. French privateers began to attack American merchant ships on the open sea, as the U.S. and France became involved in an undeclared naval war between 1798 and 1800. Anger over this and other French actions

16

and fears about losing the presidential election of 1800 led the Adams administration to accept passage of the Alien and Sedition Acts in 1798.

The Alien Act lengthened the time necessary for naturalization as a citizen, from 5 to 14 years. The Sedition Act made it possible for people to be fined or imprisoned for criticism of the U.S. government. This law restricted the First Amendment guarantees of freedom of speech and press. Thomas Jefferson and James Madison, who opposed these laws, offered the Virginia and Kentucky Resolutions in response; they raised the doctrine of "States Rights" as a way to oppose the unpopular legislation. The Alien and Sedition Acts became a major issue in the election of 1800. The acts were allowed to expire under the administration of Thomas Jefferson.

_____ 1. The first 10 amendments to the Constitution are known as A) Bill of Rights B) Preamble C) Separation of Power D) None of these listed

_____ 2. An opponent of the Alien and Sedition Acts was A) Andrew Johnson B) John Q. Adams C) Thomas Jefferson D) Thomas Jones

_____ 3. The Congress of the United States was set up by the A) Compromise of 1820 B) Connecticut Compromise C) Clay-Van Buren Agreement D) Great Awakening

_____ 4. The group that elects the President is known as the A) Electoral College B) Popular Vote C) United States Senate D) House of Representatives

_____ 5. The protest to the Alien and Sedition Acts was called A) Force Act B) Initiative and Referendum C) Virginia and Kentucky Resolutions D) Hartford Convention

_____ 6. The three branches of government include Executive, Legislative and A) Operational B) Judicial C) Legal D) Military

_____ 7. The political group that stood for strong central government was known as A) Anti-Federalists B) Federalists C) Populists D) Prohibitionists

_____ 8. The leader of the Anti-Federalists was A) Thomas Jefferson B) Alexander Hamilton C) George Washington D) Benjamin Franklin

_____ 9. The Constitution provided for a strong central government that controlled foreign policy and A) Slave rights B) Defense of the country C) Voting rights for women D) Education

_____ 10. The successor to George Washington was A) Aaron Burr B) Thomas Pinckney C) Henry Clay D) John Adams

Chapter V -- The Era of Thomas Jefferson, 1801-1824

Time Line

1800	Revolution of 1800
	Thomas Jefferson elected
	Anti-Federalists gain White House
1803	Louisiana Territory purchased from France
1808	James Madison elected President
1812	War of 1812 with England
1814	Hartford Convention
	Treaty of Ghent-End of War of 1812
1816	James Monroe elected President
1817	Henry Clay introduced the American System
1819	Adams-Onis treaty for the purchase of Florida
1823	Monroe Doctrine announced
1824	John Q. Adams elected President
	First time popular votes tabulated in presidential election

Key Terms

Civil Liberties
Inter-state Commerce
Manifest Destiny
Impressment
Agrarian Imperialism
Sectionalism
Missouri Compromise, 1820

Election of 1800

Sometimes referred to as the "Revolution of 1800", this election was a peaceful transfer of power from the Federalists to the supporters of Jefferson. After 12 years in power the party of Washington and Adams would never again win the office of President. The Federalist attack on civil liberties (the Sedition Act) cost them dearly. In the electoral college each of the electors cast two votes for Thomas Jefferson and Aaron Burr, resulting in a tie. Burr decided to challenge Jefferson for the Presidency in the House of Representatives. After several ballots Jefferson was elected. To prevent such an occurrence in the future, the 12th Amendment was passed in 1804, creating a separate ballot for President and Vice President.

John Marshall and the Supreme Court

Within this period, the United States Supreme Court under the leadership of Chief Justice John Marshall (1801-1835) established itself as the third major branch of government. In a series of important cases, the court defined the meaning of clauses in the Constitution and set the framework for the American legal system. Beginning in 1803, in Marbury v. Madison, the court stated that, under Article III, it had the power to determine whether an act of the national government and the state governments violated the U.S. Constitution; this power to determine constitutionality is called "judicial review". In the Dartmouth College v. Woodward (1817) case, it defined the "contract clause" and ruled that the state of New Hampshire could not make Dartmouth, a private college, part of the state university system. While in McCulloch v. Maryland (1819), it upheld the creation of the Bank of the United States and denied the states the right to tax the Federal Government or its agencies. In the Gibbons v. Ogden (1824) case, it asserted that only the federal government had the right to regulate interstate commerce.

Foreign Policy

The mainlines of American foreign policy were defined in this era. The main goals were securing the boundaries of the nation while removing foreign influence.

The Jefferson Administration, in 1803, purchased the Louisiana territory from France for $15 million, which doubled the size of the country.

War of 1812

That accomplished, Jefferson and his successor, James Madison became embroiled in a conflict with the British. English harassment of American merchant ships on the open sea (impressment) coupled with the sectional desires to expand into Canada led ultimately to Madison's declaration of war in 1812. The War of 1812 (1812-1815), led to the first powerful anti-war movement in American history, especially in the northeastern states. Meeting in Hartford, late in 1814, a convention threatened secession of northern states if the conflict was not ended immediately. Those in attendance were mostly New England Federalists and the party was discredited as unpatriotic when news of the war's end became known. The signing of the peace treaty took place in Ghent, Belgium late in 1814. The biggest American victory of the war came after the signing of the treaty when Andrew Jackson led his troops against the British at New Orleans; the victory transformed Jackson into a national hero. Within a few years the U.S. and England became close international partners and diplomatically settled outstanding differences.

Meanwhile, the administration of James Monroe negotiated, in 1819, the purchase of Florida from Spain, after a short military campaign by Jackson into Florida forced the issue. The Adams-Onis Treaty also secured the southeastern boundary of the country.

The successful Latin American revolutions led to the expulsion of Spain from the New World, except for Cuba and Puerto Rico, but left the former colonies vulnerable to attack by other European countries. To forestall this possibility, President James Monroe (1817-1825) issued a statement in 1823, called the Monroe Doctrine, in which the United States pledged to keep out of European affairs and told the European countries to stay out of the Western Hemisphere. However, British naval power played the key role in preventing European expansion.

Sectionalism

The concentration of slavery in the southern states and the economic growth of the country caused regional interests to vary and sometimes conflict. Nationalists like Henry Clay tried to keep the Union together despite these divisive tendencies. Clay's policy, the American System (1817), was an attempt to foster regional economic interdependency but it was rejected by southerners, like John C. Calhoun, who saw no immediate benefit to themselves. In 1819, there were 22 states, half slave and half free. Missouri's request in 1819 for statehood ignited the controversy over slave expansion into the west. In the next year, Clay introduced the Compromise of 1820. Maine was brought in as a free state and Missouri entered as a slave state, so that the balance was at least temporarily preserved. Thomas Jefferson described the situation as similar to "having the wolf by the ears," you cannot hold him and you cannot let him go.

Election of 1824

The party of Jefferson splintered and produced four candidates who represented different regions and economic and social interests. The so called "Era of Good Feelings" of one party rule (1816-1824) ended. The candidates were: Andrew Jackson (Tennessee-Frontier West); William Crawford (Virginia-South); Henry Clay (Kentucky-Border States) and John Quincy Adams (Massachusetts-North). The popular vote, tabulated for the first time, was won by Andrew Jackson. But the four candidates split the electoral vote and no one was able to win a majority so the election was decided by the House of Representatives. John Q. Adams and Henry Clay seemed to make an arrangement whereby Adams would be elected President with Clay's support and then would appoint him Secretary of State. Jackson felt cheated and stormed out of Washington. He and his supporters were determined to win the presidency in 1828.

Chapter V -- The Era of Thomas Jefferson, 1801-1824
Review Questions

_____ 1. The hero of the battle of New Orleans was A) John Adams
B) Andrew Jackson C) Robert E. Lee D) Winfield Scott

_____ 2. The Jefferson administration negotiated the purchase of the A)
Louisiana Purchase B) Gadsden Purchase C) Texas D) Florida

_____ 3. The following Supreme Court decision stated that the states could
not tax the Federal Government a) Marbury v. Madison B) Dred
Scott C) McCulloch v. Maryland D) John Marshall v. Connecticut

_____ 4. A meeting held to protest the War of 1812 was A) Hartford
Convention B) Philadelphia Caucus C) Clay-Van Buren Agreement
D) American System

_____ 5. The War of 1812 was ended with the signing of the A) Webster-
Ashburton Treaty B) Treaty of Paris C) Treaty of Ghent
D) Washington Treaty

_____ 6. The concept of Judicial Review was set forward in the case
A) Marbury v. Madison B) Fletcher v. Peck C) Gibbons v. Ogden
D) Force Act

_____ 7. A plan introduced by Henry Clay to make the various sections
more interdependent on each other was called A) American
System B) Hartford Convention C) Sectionalism D) Texas Plan

_____ 8. The election of 1812 was the last stand for the A) Whig Party
B) Federalist Party C) Republican Party D) Free Masons

_____ 9. The election of 1800 was resolved A) By the Electoral College
B) Popular Vote C) U.S. Senate D) The House of Representatives

_____ 10. The states involved in the Compromise of 1820 were A) Florida
and Georgia B) Maine and Maryland C) Maine and Missouri D)
Connecticut and Virginia

Chapter VI -- The Era of Andrew Jackson, 1828-1848

Time Line

1828   Andrew Jackson elected President as Democratic party candidate
1832   Bank recharter introduced
1836   Martin Van Buren elected President
1840   William Henry Harrison elected President as Whig
1841   John Tyler became President as Harrison died
1842   Webster-Ashburton treaty with England
1844   James K. Polk elected President
1845   Texas joins the Union
1846   Mexican War began
1848   Zachary Taylor elected President

Key Terms

Spoils System
Economic Depression
Joint Resolution of Congress
Bank of the United States
Pet Banks
Indian Removal Policy
Nullification Crisis

Andrew Jackson

Andrew Jackson scored a decisive victory over President John Quincy Adams in 1828 and changed the party's name from Democratic-Republican to Democratic. He was the first "westerner" elected to the White House and brought a vigorous presence to the national scene. Jackson was an "outsider" who had no faith in traditional politics. This he emphasized because he had been cheated out of the presidency in 1824 by the Washington "establishment". Building on his campaign slogans to protect the ordinary farmers and city workers -- the "common man" -- Jackson set out to change procedures of the national government, replacing about 10% of the employees with his loyal followers. While he defended this system as "rotation in office", his opponents termed it the "spoils system" (To the victor belongs the spoils).

Major Issues

The three great policy issues of Jackson's presidency were the Indian Removal Scheme, the Nullification Crisis and the Bank War. Although Jackson was very popular, historians still debate the wisdom of his actions.

Indian Removal

Andrew Jackson had fought Indians all his life and determined to continue the policy begun during the Monroe administration of removing all Indians east of the Mississippi River to the Oklahoma area west of the river, commonly called the "American Desert". By the end of his presidency in 1837, the forced removal of more than 15,000 Indians from the southeastern states was about to begin and the "trail of tears" was completed by his hand-picked successor, Martin Van Buren

The Nullification Crisis

The Nullification Crisis arose out of South Carolina's rejection of the 1832 tariff. Basing its actions on the states' rights theory of Jefferson as restated by John C. Calhoun in 1828, South Carolina seemed to challenge Jackson and the Union. Jackson believed that Calhoun was behind the state's action, called it treason and threatened to lead federal troops into Charleston, S.C. and hang all traitors. (Jackson had broken with Calhoun, his first Vice President). Henry Clay, who helped solve the Missouri Crisis of 1819, devised a compromise which gradually reduced the tariff rate over ten years. This ended the crisis as South Carolina repealed its ordinance of nullification while asserting the right of a state to nullify national laws.

Bank of the United States

The third issue concerned the Bank of the United States that had been created during the Washington Administration and rechartered by President James Madison in 1816. Jackson expressed contempt for all banks, but especially the Bank of the United States and vetoed the bank recharter in 1832. This became the chief issue in the election campaign of 1832 but Andrew Jackson was able to defeat Henry Clay. The government then placed its revenues in 23 "pet banks" chartered by the states. Destruction of the bank created instability in the American financial system that helped bring on an economic depression known as the "Panic of 1837". This ultimately caused grief for the administration of Van Buren, who lost his re-election bid in 1840.

The Whig Party

The opponents of Andrew Jackson led by Henry Clay became known as the "Whigs". Believing that Jackson was a tyrant, and derisively referring to him as "King Andrew I", the Whigs followers created a second major national political party. The economic depression gave them the opportunity to defeat the Democrats. They chose a military hero and Indian fighter William Henry Harrison as their victorious candidate in 1840. Their victory was short lived as Harrison died soon after being inaugurated. He was succeeded by John Tyler.

Foreign Policy

The United States relations with England continued harmoniously. In 1842, the Webster-Ashburton treaty settled the northern border of the United States and Canada from Maine to Minnesota and established the tradition of an unarmed border with Canada.

However, in the southwest trouble was developing. American citizens crossed into Texas as early as 1820, at first with the permission of the Mexican government. But the Americans opposed Mexican policies, including the prohibition of slavery. Sam Houston and Stephen Austin established the independent Republic of Texas in 1836. The Lone Star Republic existed as an independent nation from 1836-1845, while a fierce debate raged in the United States between free and slave state forces over the admittance of Texas in the Union as a slave state. It became a central issue in the election of 1844. The narrow victory of James Polk over Henry Clay persuaded Congress to accept President Tyler's request to bring Texas into the Union as a slave state. This was achieved in 1845 by a Joint Resolution of Congress.

Chapter VI -- The Era of Andrew Jackson, 1828-1848
Review Questions

_____ 1. Andrew Jackson's policy of appointing allies to office was known as A) Caucus System B) Spoils System C) Civil Service D) Economic Assistance

_____ 2. The diplomatic negotiations that settled the boundary line between Maine and Canada was A) Webster-Ashburton Treaty B) Adams-Onis Treaty C) Treaty of London D) None of the above

_____ 3. The Mexican War was fought over the issue of A) Texas B) Puerto Rico C) Central America D) Florida

_____ 4 The Bank Recharter Bill of 1832 aimed at the destruction of A) Pet Banks B) Bank of the United States C) Independent Banks D) Van Buren Bank

_____ 5. The political party that rose in opposition to Andrew Jackson was the A) Anti Federalist B) Whig C) Democratic D) Free-Mason

_____ 6. Andrew Jackson was the first President to be elected who came from the A) West B) South C) North D) Canadian Border

_____ 7. The leader in South Carolina during the nullification crisis was A) John Calhoun B) John Q. Adams C) Henry Clay D) Andrew Johnson

_____ 8. The Lone Star Republic was finally admitted as a state in 1845 known as A) California B) Texas C) Utah D) North Carolina

_____ 9. The nullification crisis arose out of South Carolina's rejection of A) Tariff of 1832 B) Slavery C) Compromise of 1820 D) Election of 1832

_____10. Andrew Jackson was said to represent the A) Farmers B) Common Man C) Washington Insiders D) Diplomats

Chapter VII -- Economic Change, Westward Expansion and Sectional Discord, 1820-1860

Time Line

1846   Wilmot Proviso introduced in Congress
1848   Seneca Falls Convention - Women's Rights
        Treaty of Guadalupe-Hidalgo - end of Mexican War

Key Terms

Great Awakening
Perfectionism
Abolitionism

Background

Between 1815 and 1860 the United States economically transformed itself from an agricultural nation of about 9 million into an urban, industrial giant of 32 million. One major byproduct of this change was the creation of major tensions between the north and south over a variety of issues.

Economic Changes

The United States Government provided a framework of peace and order enabling the rapidly growing American population to exploit the abundant natural resources (fertile soil, timber, iron, coal, copper, lead and water power) and develop farms, factories, cities, transportation systems, and so on. Inexpensive land acted as a magnet drawing people westward and encouraged the swift application of new technologies (like steam power) to transportation, giving rise to a network of roads, rivers serviced by steamboats, and railroads between 1800 and 1850. Between 1830 and 1850 railroads made it possible for each section within America to specialize in the production of those goods it could produce best.

The northeast specialized in manufacturing, trade, commerce, and financial services, while the south focused on producing and exporting cotton and tobacco and a new section, the west, became the main producer and shipper of foodstuffs as well as minerals, like copper, iron, coal, and so on; before too long the west also became a manufacturer of iron and steel for use in railroad construction.

28

The north and west were tied together by the transportation network and by strong economic, social and political bonds, while the southerners felt increasingly isolated.

Religion and Reform

As the economic changes began to take hold, in the 1820's, revivalism ignited a religious fervor all over the nation, called the Great Awakening, but it was most pronounced in the northeast and west. Its principal ingredient was the belief in "perfectionism" which helped kindle many different reform movements and changed existing institutions, practices and customs. Perfectionism held that sincere Christians, irrespective of denomination, could effect their own salvation by perfecting themselves and their society's institutions.

Social reformism in the United States had its beginnings in this pre-civil war period. Americans sought to eliminate vices, like alcohol, from society, reform prisons, build mental asylums, create free public school systems, and so on. Women played an extremely significant role in both the religious revivalism and these social reform activities.

Horace Mann and Henry Barnard led the drive for the establishment of free public education in the cities of the north. Women's rights advocates began to work for voting rights, legal equality with men, and equality of opportunity. In 1848 Elizabeth Cady Stanton, Lucretia Mott and Susan B. Anthony organized a conference for women's rights at Seneca Falls, N.Y. Dorothea Dix led the fight for more humane treatment for the mentally ill, and several states established asylums for their treatment.

The Abolition Movement

Perfectionism also helped fuel the anti-slavery movement which was the most controversial of all the reforms. While some abolitionists (as they were called) believed slavery should be ended gradually and with compensation to the slaveowners, they were outnumbered by those who wanted the immediate and total end of slavery in America. Though the abolitionists were a tiny minority in the north and west, they endlessly repeated their simple message over almost thirty years, so that by 1860 all Americans knew it. Slavery, they stated, was a sin; slavery was incompatible with the American way of life; slavery was a brutal and brutalizing institution, brutalizing the slaves and the masters; and that southerners would do anything to protect slavery in America.

The refusal of the northern state governments and people to silence the abolitionists infuriated most southerners who saw this as another evidence of northern hostility.

The South, 1800-1860

The South was as diverse an area as any other section of the United States, for its climatic, topographical, and geographical conditions varied widely across the 11 states comprising the region. This variety was reflected in the crops grown (including corn, its leading crop; cotton, its greatest cash crop; tobacco; hemp, for rope; sugar; and rice) and industries (including textile mills, mining, timber, construction, and some steel mills). What made the southern way of life unique - and unified the south -- was the concentration there of more than four million African-American slaves. Slavery was simultaneously a form of racial domination, a labor system and the foundation upon which arose a distinctive ruling class within the south. Fears about the impact of ending slavery -- or slave uprisings -- drove the 75% of the white population who owned no slaves to support the leadership of the 25% of the whites who owned all the slaves.

Southern slaveholders as different as George Washington, Thomas Jefferson, Andrew Jackson, John C. Calhoun and Alexander Stephens justified human slavery in a variety of ways. They claimed that it was sanctioned in the Bible, that every society had slaves, that slavery was a "positive good" for southern whites and blacks, but mainly they argued that blacks were inherently inferior to whites because of race. Some of them were convinced that slavery in America could not be ended unless, in Jefferson's words, "emancipation" was accompanied by "expatriation" (sending the African-Americans out of the country). Alexander Stephens would proudly assert in March 1861 that slavery was the "cornerstone" of the southern confederacy and protection of it was the reason the south seceded from the union in 1860-1861.

Westward Expansion and Sectional Divisions

It was westward expansion across the continent and the acquisition of new territories that brought the north and south into collision. This had begun with Missouri's request for entry into the union in 1819 and erupted explosively over Texas annexation and the subsequent Mexican War.

The loss of Texas was very difficult for the Mexicans to accept. President James Polk sought to obtain California from Mexico and manipulated the situation in 1846. He used a pretext to ask Congress to declare War. Divisions over the war in the United States were intense, especially in New England. Evidence of this was the furor over the Wilmot Proviso introduced in Congress in 1846 and 1847. It would have banned slavery in any western territories the U.S. might obtain from Mexico, but it was blocked by southern senators. However, it did mark the beginning of a new and extremely explosive division over the extension of slavery into the west.

The Mexican War, 1846-1848

The Americans had little trouble winning the war, despite the political opposition in the country. It turned out to be a training ground for army officers who would later command large armies in the Civil War. Under the leadership of Zachary Taylor and Winfield Scott, the Mexicans were decisively defeated. A peace treaty was signed in the small Mexican town of Guadalupe-Hidalgo in 1848. Mexico formally ceded Texas, New Mexico, Arizona parts of Utah and California and the United States gave Mexico 15 million dollars and assumed the debts of American citizens owed by Mexico.

Although the war was swift and decisive, its effects would take a terrible toll on the United States.

Chapter VII -- Economic Change, Westward Expansion and Sectional Discord, 1820-1860
Review Questions

_____ 1. A crusader for improved treatment of the insane was A) Horace Mann B) Henry Barnard C) Henrietta Wilson D) Dorothea Dix

_____ 2 The Mexican war officially ended with the treaty signed at A) London B) Mexico City C) Washington D) Guadalupe-Hidalgo

_____ 3. The religious revivalism that spread across the U.S. was known as A) Great Awakening B) New Lights C) Regionalism D) Fundamentalism

_____ 4. Those who believed that slavery should be ended immediately were A) Perfectionists B) Abolitionists C) Slaveryites D) Reconstructionists

_____ 5. A convention held for women's rights met in A) Hartford B) Springfield C) Seneca Falls D) Montreal

_____ 6. Southern cash crops included all but A) Tobacco B) Cotton C) Cattle Raising D) Rice

_____ 7. A leading American general in the Mexican War was A) Winfield Scott B) U.S. Grant C) Ethan Allen D) Robert E. Lee

_____ 8. A leading proponent of slavery was A) Alexander Stephens B) William Garrison C) Sara Grimke D) Dorothea Dix

_____ 9. The American President in office when the Mexican War began was A) Martin Van Buren B) James K. Polk C) James Buchanan D) Andrew Jackson

_____ 10. This was introduced in Congress to try and block the expansion of slavery into the western territories A) Ostend Manifesto B) Wilmot Proviso C) Adams-Onis D) American System

Chapter VIII -- The Coming of War, 1848-1860

Time Line

1850   Millard Fillmore became President after death of Zachary Taylor
        Compromise of 1850 adopted
1852   Franklin Pierce Elected President
1854   Ostend Manifesto Proposed
        Kansas-Nebraska Act
1856   James Buchanan elected President
1857   Dred Scott Case
1858   Lincoln-Douglas Debates

Key Terms

Popular Sovereignty
Fugitive Slave
Personal Liberty Law
Bleeding Kansas
Gold Rush 1849

The Coming of War 1848-1860

The discovery of gold in California in January 1848 created a rush by January 1849 to get there. It also led to the demand for California's immediate entry as a state. The struggle between north and south over expansion of slavery flared again.

Compromise of 1850

The demand for California's statehood created a crisis in Congress and Henry Clay devised a last ditch compromise to hold the Union together. This became the Compromise of 1850.

Although there was much debate and anger over the proposals, they were finally passed with the aid of Sen. Stephen A. Douglas of Illinois. The provisions were: California entered the Union as a free state; the new western territories would enter under the doctrine of popular sovereignty (people in the territories would choose slavery or freedom before statehood); the slave trade would be abolished in Washington, D.C.; and there would be a strict new fugitive slave law.

Extremists on both sides did not like the agreement, but they did not have enough votes in Congress to sabotage the compromise.

Fugitive Slave Law

All the south received in the compromise was the new fugitive slave law, but northern people refused to implement it. To counter the new law many northern states passed "Personal Liberty" laws which stated that anyone entering a northern state was a free person and not to be stopped by local authorities. Northerners had grown up on anti-slave works like <u>Uncle Tom's Cabin</u> by Harriet Beecher Stowe and considered slavery wrong, although they were not necessarily sympathetic to African-Americans in their midst.

Ostend Manifesto

Southerners were convinced that the possibility of adding new slave states from western lands obtained from Mexico was bleak and began to look for alternatives. In 1854, three American diplomats met in Ostend, Belgium and issued the Ostend Manifesto. They wanted the United States to seize Cuba and bring it into the Union as a slave state. President Franklin Pierce rejected the manifesto and the idea was dropped. It demonstrated, however, the desperation of the pro-slave forces.

Kansas-Nebraska Act

The doctrine of popular sovereignty received its first test with the passage of the Kansas-Nebraska Act in 1854. Arranged by Stephen A. Douglas, the act was designed to open the vast Nebraska area (comprising the present Kansas and Nebraska) but southern senators forced a compromise that insured one of the areas would be a slave state. Thus the Missouri compromise was repealed and Kansas became a battleground between pro and anti slave forces. A seven year civil war known as "Bleeding Kansas" erupted. In August 1858, the people of Kansas voted overwhelmingly against slavery in a referendum. Finally, in 1862, during the Civil War, President Lincoln brought Kansas into the Union as a free state.

The Dred Scott Case, 1857

In 1857, in the midst of the Kansas problem, the Supreme Court issued its decision in the Dred Scott case. Dred Scott was a slave who was used as a personal servant by an army physician. He had been taken to Illinois which was a free state and had a personal liberty law and then returned to Missouri which was a slave state. Scott sued for his freedom with the help of abolitionists. He claimed he was a resident of a free state and therefore was a free person. The case ultimately went to the Supreme Court where the justices ruled against him. Adding to the problem, in 1857, the Supreme Court issued its decision in the Dred Scott Case. Chief Justice, Roger Taney, a southern slaveholder, insisted in the decision that a slave was not a citizen because slaves were not people but personal property. Taney argued that Congress did not have the authority under the Fifth Amendment of the Constitution to ban slavery from the western territories as it had in the Missouri Compromise of 1820. While southerners praised the decision, northerners viewed it as an attack on their way of life.

Abraham Lincoln and the Republican Party

Abraham Lincoln became a national leader in the late 1850's as a consequence of the slavery issue. The north-south split within the Whig party over the expansion of slavery finally killed the party; the furor over the Kansas-Nebraska Act was the last straw. A new anti-slavery Republican party emerged which Lincoln helped create, in 1854. It drew its strength from northern Whigs and Democrats who opposed the southern domination of their party. In the presidential election of 1856, the Democratic candidate, Pennsylvania Senator James Buchanan comfortably won the election, but the Republican candidate drew more than one million votes in the northern states. Lincoln emerged as a national figure while losing a senatorial election against Stephen Douglas in 1858. In his speeches and a series of campaign debates in Illinois, Lincoln made his views against slavery known. He stated that the country could not continue to exist half slave and half free. Moreover, Lincoln called for the "ultimate extinction" of slavery in North America. This position made him and the Republican party totally unacceptable to the south.

_____ 1. The compromise of 1850 was drawn up by A) John Calhoun
B) Daniel Webster C) Henry Clay D) Robert Moore

_____ 2. A provision of the 1850 Compromise was that the slave trade in
Washington, D.C. would be A) Made legal B) Suspended C)
Abolished D) Stay as it was

_____ 3. These laws were passed by northern states to try and get around
the new fugitive slave law A) Force Act B) Personal Liberty Law C)
Exemption Law D) Expansion Act

_____ 4. A leading anti-slave author of the pre-civil war era was A) Harriet
Beecher Stowe B) Lyman Beecher C) James Fenimore Cooper D)
Frank Norris

_____ 5. New territories entering the Union would be subject to the doctrine
of A) Immediate Entry B) Filibuster C) Monroe Doctrine
D) Popular Sovereignty

_____ 6. An outgrowth of the fugitive slave law was the Supreme Court
case that involved A) Horace Mann B) Dred Scott C) Harriet
Taubman D) Hinton Helper

_____ 7. The passage of this act led to virtual civil war in the territories
A) California Compromise B) Wilmot Proviso C) Kansas-Nebraska
D) Lincoln-Douglas Act

_____ 8. A southern attempt to add new slave territory can be seen in A)
Ostend Manifesto B) Kansas-Nebraska C) Georgia Pacific D)
Intolerable Act

_____ 9. The Chief Justice of the Supreme Court at this time was
A) Thurgood Marshall B) Hinton Helper C) Roger Taney
D) Henry Clay

_____ 10. The death of the Whig Party gave birth to a new anti-slave party
A) Democratic-Republican Party B) Free Soil Party
C) Republican D) Charter Oak Party

<u>Time Line</u>

1861	Abraham Lincoln sworn in as President
	Southern states secede from Union
	Civil War began
1863	Union victory at Gettysburg
1865	Civil War ends at Appomattox Court House
	Abraham Lincoln Assassinated
	Reconstruction began
	Andrew Johnson sworn in as President
1867	Tenure of Office Act
	Impeachment of Andrew Johnson
1868	Election of U.S. Grant as President
1876	Election of Rutherford Hayes as President
1877	Compromise of 1877 ended Reconstruction

<u>Key Terms</u>

Secession
Confederacy
Anaconda Policy
Reconstruction
Impeachment

<u>Secession</u>

The election of 1860 proved to militant southerners that the Federal Government would not protect slavery. This issue split the Democratic party and produced two candidates with opposing views on slavery. In addition, former Whig party members in the south ran their own candidate as the Union party. Despite this division, the Republican candidate, Abraham Lincoln, was able to win the election, although he failed to gain a majority of the popular votes.

<u>Electoral</u>		<u>Popular</u>	
Lincoln(Rep.)	180	Lincoln	1,866,352
Breckinridge (S.D.)	72	Douglas	1,375,157
Bell (Union)	39	Breckinridge	845,763
Douglas	12	Bell	589,881

Southerners viewed Lincoln's election as a mandate to secede from the Union. The southern states, except for Delaware, Kentucky, Maryland and Missouri) left the Union and created the Confederate States of America. (West Virginia broke away from Virginia and became a state in 1863). In April 1861, the Confederates under the leadership of Jefferson Davis attacked Fort Sumter (S.C.) and the Civil War began.

Military Tactics

Superior Union resources and industrial power ultimately gave the North the margin of victory. At first both sides underestimated the ability of the other. Southerners had the advantage of being on the defensive and fought most of the war on familiar territory. However, modern technological advances in warfare and weaponry made old tactics obsolete and resulted in very high casualty rates.

Initial Confederate successes, under the leadership of General Robert E. Lee between1861-1862, gradually stalled as the Union was able to implement its own plan. The Anaconda policy called for a blockade by the U.S. Navy to prevent foreign supplies from reaching the Confederacy. Admiral Farragut captured the port of New Orleans which effectively isolated Texas, the food-producing area of the Confederacy. Under the command of two Union generals, U.S. Grant and William T. Sherman, the Confederates were pushed back into a concentrated area. An escape attempt by Robert E. Lee and his army resulted in the battle of Gettysburg in July 1863. Lee's army was defeated and forced to retreat back to Virginia. Two more years of fighting finally resulted in a Confederate surrender at Appomattox Court House in Virginia (1865).

Reconstruction

Reconstruction was the rebuilding of the South at the end of the war. But reconciliation and forgiveness did not easily follow four bloody years of war. Before his assassination in April 1865, President Abraham Lincoln put forward a conciliatory plan to restore the southern states to the Union. But his successor, Andrew Johnson, a Southern Democrat who remained loyal to the Union, did not have Lincoln's prestige or support and dramatically changed the plan by granting pardons to thousands of high ranking Confederate officers and planters. While Lincoln was sympathetic to the needs of the close to four million ex-slaves, Johnson shared southern attitudes toward African-Americans. Although Johnson supported the passage of the 13th Amendment to the Constitution in 1865 (ending slavery), he opposed Congress' other efforts to guarantee freedmen's rights. Because of this disagreement, in 1868 Congress passed the 14th Amendment, granting citizenship to the former slaves. The last of the so-called Civil War amendments was the formulation of the 15th Amendment which granted the former slaves the right to vote. It was ratified in 1870.

Impeachment

As President, Andrew Johnson was in charge of administering the Reconstruction program but was seen by northern Republicans as a hindrance to its implementation. The Tenure of Office Act was the legislation the congressional majority passed to weaken the President's authority. This act prohibited him from removing civil officials, even Cabinet members, without the Senate's consent. In August 1867, President Johnson dismissed Secretary of War Stanton even though the Senate had refused to approve his action.

Congressional Republicans in the House impeached Andrew Johnson, charging him with violating the Tenure of Office Act, slandering the Congress, and not enforcing the Reconstruction Acts. The breach between Congress and the southern President was so deep, removal of the Chief Executive seemed possible. However, Johnson was saved by one vote in the Senate.

Radical Reconstruction

The majority of southern whites adamantly refused to accept former slaves as citizens or even potential citizens of the U.S., despite the passage of the 13th, 14th and 15th Amendments, and tenaciously fought, politically and with violence, to maintain southern "white supremacy". Northerners who came south, most to help, some to take advantage of the conditions, were called "carpetbaggers", while white southerners who helped the northerners were called "scalawags". Under the protection of Union soldiers, there were some useful projects that were carried out during the period 1865-1877; public school systems were created in the south for the first time; economic diversification projects were begun and hundreds of miles of railroad tracks were laid. But the combination of southern hostility and northern disillusionment caused the collapse of reconstruction policies based in large part on protecting the rights of African-Americans. Americans became diverted by other issues, such as westward expansion and industrial development. Or they became disillusioned by the seeming failure of blacks to make greater progress. Meanwhile, former slaves were falling backward into a system of dependency called share cropping and debt peonage, or as it came to be known, "Jim Crow Segregation", that would last into the 1960's.

End of Reconstruction

The election of 1876 brought Republican Rutherford Hayes to the Presidency. The Hayes administration sought to end reconstruction so that the country might get on with the business at hand which was industrialization. Therefore, the Compromise of 1877 brought the era to a conclusion. Southern Democrats agreed to cooperate with the new Republican President. Union soldiers were removed from the south and a southerner was appointed to a cabinet position in the new administration.

underlying factors responsible for this spectacular economic growth: Millions of foreign immigrants (between 1880 and 1914, about 20 million) entered the United States and provided a tremendous pool of cheap labor; vast amounts of capital, both foreign and domestic, was available for investment in American industries; and Americans possessed enormous amounts of high quality mineral resources for development. Another important factor was the close cooperation between the American government and the business community.

Captains of Industry

The partnership between business and national corporate leaders produced a new class of businessmen. National corporate leaders like Cornelius Vanderbilt, James Duke, Andrew Carnegie and J.P. Morgan became extraordinarily rich and powerful. Although the government cooperated with business enterprise, it did not in significant ways regulate how these new national businesses operated. The absence of government regulations allowed these capitalists free reign without any concern for the general welfare of workers or American society in general. These captains of industry used any means possible to dispose of their competition. Many of the nationwide businesses became monopolies controlled by one corporation. Quite a few of these business leaders became widely known as "Robber Barons" because of their business practices.

Problems of Workers

Labor had no economic or political leverage and made few gains until the 20th century. It became apparent to many workers that the hostility of management and government could only be overcome by strong labor unions. Most workers were poorly paid. There were no regulations regarding working conditions. Workers were usually crowded into slum sections of industrial cities and forced to live in poor housing. The Knights of Labor led by Terence Powderly grew rapidly and by 1886 had about 700,000 members comprised of skilled and unskilled laborers. Their complex goals included support of the 8 hour work day, the abolition of child labor and a variety of non-labor related issues. A new union emerged in the 1880's called the American Federation of Labor (AFL) which was led by Samuel Gompers and composed exclusively of skilled workers. It succeeded in its labor-related goals and by 1900 had about 500,000 members.

Government and the Courts

The Federal government and the courts took an anti-union position between 1876-1900. As early as 1877, in a national railroad strike, the courts came down on the side of the corporations. Court orders (called injunctions) forbade union activity and made unionists law breakers. These damaging court actions were upheld by the Supreme Court. At the same time corporate leaders used strike breakers, private detectives and spies as weapons to try and break unions. This anti-union position would not be changed until the 1930's.

Political Reform

Declining farm prices, drought and poor conditions for workers led to the development of a new political party. The Peoples Party (Populists), consisting of a coalition of mid-western farmers and southern planters came onto the political scene in 1890. The Populist Party platform was designed to break the power of the political bosses and give the masses more effective control of the government. Among their demands were the following: The 8 hour work day; government control of the railroads; direct election of senators; and a graduated income tax. However, many of their objectives, including national workers cooperatives, proved too complex to implement. In 1892, the Populists ran a candidate in the presidential election. While they polled more than 1 million popular votes, it was not nearly enough to win. The party eventually merged with the Democratic Party in 1896. In spite of that alliance, Ohio Republican William McKinley won the election.

corruption by business, robber barons and politicians in leading magazines and newspapers. Among the most famous of these journalists was Ray Stannard Baker, Ida Tarbell, and Lincoln Steffens. Upton Sinclair's book, The Jungle described the meat packing industry and it led to the passage of the Meat Inspection Act (1906) and its companion the Pure Food and Drug Act (1908).

Presidential Politics

President Theodore Roosevelt (1902-1909) moved away from governmental support of big corporations in the Coal Strike (1903), siding with the workers and consumers, and directed the breakup of the Northern Securities Company (1903). This was the first successful prosecution of a monopoly under the Sherman Anti-Trust Act passed in 1890. Roosevelt was the first President who sought to protect the nation's public lands from ceaseless development and established what became the national parks system. Inspired by President Roosevelt's activism, progressives sought to end boss rule and political machines at the state and local levels and to pass social legislation of all kinds, such as unemployment insurance and compensation to workers who had been injured on the job.

William H. Taft (1909-1913) directed his Attorney General to prosecute more than 90 anti-trust (monopoly) cases. Also, Congress expanded the powers of the Interstate Commerce Commission (Elkins Act 1910) to regulate business on the nation's railroads and roads. Continuing Roosevelt's efforts, the Taft administration advocated leasing public lands (for harvests of timber) rather than selling to private developers.

When Roosevelt decided to challenge Taft for the Presidency in the election of 1912, the Democratic candidate Woodrow Wilson was able to squeeze out a narrow victory as President. Under Wilson's New Freedom program, progressivism continued and four constitutional amendments were enacted: the 16th authorized a graduated income tax; the 17th provided for direct election of senators; the 18th prohibited the manufacture and sale of alcoholic beverages (above the alcoholic content of 3.2%), and the 19th authorized women the right to vote in national elections.

The Underwood Tariff was the first major reduction in import duties since the end of the Civil War (1913) and in 1914 the monetary system was stabilized with the passage of the Federal Reserve Act.

Wilson was narrowly reelected in 1916. His second term was marked by his preoccupation with foreign policy matters including the first World War.

America Becomes a World Power 1900-1920

In the years following the Civil War American energies were directed at dealing with internal matters and foreign policy was all but ignored. The 1890's, however, witnessed the American involvement in both Latin America and the Far East. From the 1870's on the European nations sought to obtain colonies or 'spheres of influence' in Asia and Latin America. This flexing of military and naval power by England, Germany and Japan made some American leaders feel less secure. Quietly, the U.S. fleet was transformed from a merely defensive force to a modern fleet second in size to England and Germany.

Spanish-American War, 1898-1900

A ten year war for Cuban independence (1868-1878) ended unsuccessfully. The rebellion broke out again in 1895 and the brutality of the fighting raised genuine concern in the United States. American newspaper owners William Randolph Hearst and Joseph Pulitzer engaged in a circulation war, played up the violence and urged the U.S. government to intervene and free the Cubans. By 1898 there was considerable support for the war with Spain on humanitarian grounds mingled with a desire to flex American power.

When in 1898 the American Battleship Maine accidentally blew up in Havana harbor, the demand for war seemed unavoidable. Congress was convinced it was not an accident and President McKinley urged war. Within less than one year, the American army had taken Cuba and Puerto Rico. The navy captured the Philippine Islands. American battlefield casualties were only 300 but more than 3000 succumbed from disease. Far more soldiers were killed, however, between 1900-1902 fighting Philippine nationalists who sought independence from both Spain and the United States. This "insurrection" was American's first overseas guerrilla war.

The Treaty of Paris (1900) formally ended the war. Spain ceded title to Cuba, Puerto Rico, Guam and the Philippine Islands. The United States had now become the possessor of overseas colonies for the first time.

Caribbean 1898-1934

Using bases in Cuba, the Caribbean became a virtual lake for the U.S. Navy. American presidents, while engaged in domestic reform activities, were quite willing to use military force to protect American 'interests' in the

Chapter XII -- From World War to Economic Depression, 1917-1929

Time Line

1918   World War I ends
1919   Treaty of Paris is signed at Versailles
        19th Amendment enacted
        Women have the right to vote
1920   Warren Harding elected President
1923   Calvin Coolidge succeeds Harding as President
1924   Calvin Coolidge elected President
1928   Herbert Hoover elected President
1929   Stock market crash
        Beginning of Great Depression

Key Terms

Stock Market
Selective Service System
Zimmerman Note
Prohibition
Margin
14 Points
League of Nations

Background to War

European nations had established alliances to protect themselves and their interests. It was, in large part, this alliance system that pulled the European continent into war in 1914. The Central Powers (Germany, Austria-Hungary) were opposed by the Allies (England, France and Russia). American policy at first was one of official neutrality. However, President Wilson, the shaper of public opinion was definitely pro-British and French. Strong ties between England and the United States, both cultural and economic, had grown steadily since the turn of the century.

America Enters the War

The American policy of selling goods to any belligerent that would come and take them up was actually a boon to the Allies. England had a very strong navy and merchant fleet. To stop this flow of material to the Allies the

Germans began a policy of unrestricted submarine warfare in 1915. This resulted in the sinking of many ships including passenger vessels (<u>Lusitania</u>) and boats registered in the United States. These attacks greatly angered the Americans. In addition, the Germans tried to entice Mexican into siding with them against the United States. The Zimmerman Note promised a return of former Mexican territory in exchange for opposition to the Americans. The United States finally declared war in April 1917.

United States at War

America immediately mobilized for all out war. The Selective Service Act set up the draft. More than 2 million young men were called into military service. The Wilson administration entered into a virtual partnership with big business to ensure that wartime production quotas were met. Intolerance was the most chilling aspect of wartime America on the homefront. Popular hostility to all things German swept the country.

Military Operations

General John J. Pershing was the commander of the American Expeditionary Force (AEF) in France. The new troops, although inexperienced, were full of confidence and spirit. Their gradual infusion into the Allied ranks was one of the reasons the Germans stalled their advance and the war came to an end in 1918. The Germans surrendered but not before more than 100,000 American soldiers were killed in the fighting.

Peace Conference

President Wilson went to the peace conference with his plan to ensure a lasting peace. It became known as the 14 Points. Included in this was a League of Nations. The treaty was signed at Versailles in 1919 and Wilson returned to the United States to try and seek Senate ratification of the treaty. There was considerable opposition based on feelings that the treaty limited America's freedom of action. While in the process of campaigning to change public opinion and Senate opposition, Woodrow Wilson suffered a stroke and lapsed into a semi-coma. The treaty was never approved and the United States did not join the League of Nations.

Chapter XIII -- Depression and the New Deal, 1929-1940

Time Line

1932 Franklin D. Roosevelt elected President
1933 New Deal plan announced by Roosevelt
1933 New Deal I: AAA; WPA; NRA; PWA; FERA
1935 New Deal II: Social Security; Wagner Act; CCC
1938 Fair Labor Standards Act

Key Terms

Bank Failure
Bi-Partisan
F.D.I.C.
Public Works
Fireside Chats
Welfare

Results of the Stock Market Crash

The worst economic crisis in American history began late in 1929 and lasted into the 1940's. The collapse of the stock market in 1929 wiped out about $30 billion worth of paper wealth. Its impact on the economy was real. Business slashed investment, expansion ceased and inventories grew at a rapid rate. Widespread layoffs resulted. By the mid-1930's, almost 40% of the American workforce was unemployed without a safety net to rely on for food, clothing and shelter. As unemployment spread, frightened consumers cut back on their spending, causing even more cutbacks in production and employment. Brokerage companies which had borrowed huge sums of money from banks to lend to stock purchasers defaulted on their payments. Therefore, financial institutions across the nation closed their doors and went bankrupt, wiping out millions of ordinary American's savings accounts. At the time, there was no protection for individual savings accounts if a bank defaulted. More than 4300 banks failed, industrial production fell by 48%, and farm prices dropped by more than 60%.

Election of 1932

Blamed for the depression by most Americans, Herbert Hoover faced a difficult campaign in 1932. Slogans like, "In God We Trusted; in Hoover We Busted" appeared. Unemployed people lived in shack cities called

"Hoovervilles". The Democratic candidate, Franklin Roosevelt, called for an increase in Federal spending to ease the depression. He was elected in a landslide and carried more than 40 states.

Franklin D. Roosevelt 1933-1945

A member of an old, wealthy Dutch-descended family, Roosevelt (a cousin of Theodore Roosevelt) had been Assistant Secretary of the Navy during World War I. In 1928 he had been elected Governor of New York state. Little in his background and previous experience suggested that he would be able to help a desperate nation survive a catastrophe. In retrospect, historians point to one factor that did distinguish him from other ambitious, wealthy young politicians. In the 1920's he contracted polio which left him unable to walk under his own power. This experience may have enabled him to identify and feel for the less successful in American society. His wife, Eleanor, became the eyes, ears, legs and heart of his administration in Albany and later on in Washington. He was able to assemble a staff of highly competent individuals with diverse views and a wealth of experience in solving problems.

The New Deal

In his inaugural address Roosevelt promised a "New Deal for the American people". Because of the scope of the economic crisis in 1933, the President received bi-partisan support to handle the emergency. Legislation was speedily drafted to deal with three areas: immediate relief of the national suffering, recovery from the national economic crisis, and reform to ensure that such a crisis would not occur again.

Roosevelt sought to achieve these goals through an unusual blend of presidential activism, in part to restore national confidence, and legislation to remedy the problems. He reassured Americans of the safety of the banking system in the first of a series of radio conversations known as "Fireside Chats", while Congress passed the Emergency Banking Act and later the Federal Deposit Insurance Company (FDIC) designed to protect individual bank accounts.

To put workers back to work such laws as the Works Projects Administration (WPA) and Public Works Administration (PWA) were passed. They provided public funds to build schools, hospitals, post offices, parks, and hydro-electric dams all over the nation.

The Agricultural Adjustment Act (AAA) was aimed at restoring farmers' purchasing power by restricting farm production, until prices increased, and simultaneously paying them to plant certain soil enriching crops.

The Home Owners Loan Corporation (HOLC) helped at least one million families who otherwise would have lost their homes by providing refinanced home mortgages at low interest rates.

Other legislation included the National Recovery Act (NRA) which sought to promote national recovery through a suspension of the anti-trust laws, industry-wide codes of conduct, and Section 7A of the law enabling labor unions legally to engage in collective bargaining with management.

To help remove unemployed city youth from all sorts of temptation during the national emergency, the New Deal administration obtained passage of the Civilian Conservation Corps which set up camps for young men to work on a wide variety of rural conservation projects.

FDR, as he was increasingly called, was determined to focus his administration's efforts toward those disadvantaged people, workers and farmers. His critics claimed his efforts were motivated to help him and his party win the election of 1936. Under his leadership, there can be little doubt, the national government not only helped transform the lives of millions of people but also helped whole regions of the country. Three such actions which have had enduring effect are:

The Tennessee Valley Authority (TVA) which combined construction of a system of dams throughout the Tennessee Valley to prevent flooding and also provide inexpensive electrical power to the people in this largely rural and considered the poorest area of the nation. The Social Security Act (1935) established the first national system of unemployment insurance and pensions for workers at age 65. The Wagner Act (1936) which guaranteed the legality of collective bargaining rights for workers in trade unions. This act was passed after the Supreme Court had declared the National Recovery Act unconstitutional.

Second Term

Roosevelt defeated the Republican candidate Alfred "Alf" Landon by carrying 46 of the 48 states in 1936. During the second administration Roosevelt and the national government continued to struggle to end the depression, but as late as 1937 FDR stated "one third" of the nation was still "ill housed, ill clothed, and ill fed". Another law directed at this problem was the Fair Labor Standards Act that set up the first minimum wage for workers in companies that were engaged in interstate commerce; 40 cents an hour for a 40 hour work week. The $16 weekly wage increased the salaries of more than 50% of those affected, but still millions remained unemployed.

Despite these efforts, however, it was the economic boom sparked by World War II, not the New Deal, that finally pulled the nation out of the great depression.

Foreign Policy

Absorbed in domestic affairs, Roosevelt paid scant attention to foreign policy issues. One exception was the United States recognition of the Soviet Union in 1933. Another was the administration's effort to try and cultivate a better relationship with Latin America. Calling it the "Good Neighbor" policy, Roosevelt repudiated military interventionism and in return hoped for better trade and diplomatic relations with Latin American peoples and governments. For the most part, the policy did work because most of the Latin American governments were allies of the United States during the Second World War.

During the 1930's the rise of aggressive dictatorships in Germany, Italy and Japan led by Adolf Hitler, Benito Mussolini, and the Emperor Hirohito raised the specter of war in Europe and Asia where American had significant national interests. Preoccupied with internal concerns most Americans had little interest in the outside world. Congress responded to this seeming isolationist sentiment with the passage of neutrality legislation in 1937.

and accepted the Atlantic Charter. They pledged to fight until the Axis enemy had been defeated

America at War

American domestic industrial production was put on a wartime footing. Although twelve million able-bodied workers were sent to the armed forces, their places were taken by women and those men unfit for military service plus retirees.

Prices and wages were frozen on the homefront. With so great an emphasis on military production, civilian needs were secondary. Therefore a program of rationing went into effect. Gasoline, rubber tires and food were rationed to each family on a basis of need.

Military Strategy

The allies military strategy was coordinated by the leaders of the "Big Three" countries: Franklin D. Roosevelt (United States), Winston Churchill (England) and Joseph Stalin (Russia). They met several times (Casablanca, Teheran, Yalta, Potsdam) during the war to plan operations.

European Theatre of Operations (ETO)

American forces landed in Morocco and Tunisia in November 1942. Under the command of Dwight Eisenhower the allied forces liberated North Africa in May 1943. This was followed by attacks into Italy which finally brought down the dictatorship of Benito Mussolini.

Air power alone was not enough to defeat Germany and therefore a troop invasion was planned. On June 6, 1944 (D-Day) allied forces landed in France at Normandy. Fighting continued with the Americans and the British advancing through Western Europe into Germany. The Russians moved through Eastern Europe at the same time and entered Germany from the opposite direction.

The final offensive began in February 1945. At the end of April Adolf Hitler committed suicide. The Germans surrendered on May 8, 1945.

Pacific Theatre of Operations (PTO)

American forces gradually regained their strength after the naval fleet was virtually destroyed at Pearl Harbor. Through 1942 only minor operations against the Japanese were launched. Under the command of General Douglas MacArthur offensive strategy grew bolder and a key naval victory stopped the Japanese at Midway Island. It became a matter of island hopping to get closer to the Japanese Islands. During the Spring of 1945 Japanese coastal cities were under intense air attack from the U.S. Air Force.

After the surrender of Germany, allied power was all concentrated on Japan. The Japanese reputation for suicidal resistance led strategists to believe that an invasion of the Japanese main island would cost 1 million casualties. However, since 1942 American scientists had been at work on the Manhattan Project. This was the production of the atomic bomb. On August 6, 1945, an atomic bomb was dropped on the Japanese city of Hiroshima. Three days later another bomb was dropped on Nagasaki. On August 10, 1945, the Japanese government surrendered and the war was over.

The Holocaust

The Allies became aware of the horror and tragedy of Nazi atrocities against the Jewish people and others in Germany and areas under control of the Third Reich. Extermination of large numbers of people occurred with estimates ranging up to 6 million Jews and approximately 7 million people of varied nationalities, religious persuasions and political outlook.

Large numbers of Jewish refugees, who tried to escape the nightmare of German tyranny were turned back by the Allies, whose prime focus remained the defeat of Germany.

slip back into a period of depression. Federal spending for defense continued to help stimulate the nation's economy. It helped sustain the country's prosperity for the next five decades.

Election of 1948

It seemed that 1948 was a winning year for the Republican party. Republicans had captured control of Congress in 1945 and had a popular candidate in the Governor of New York, Thomas E. Dewey. The Democrats split over the issue of civil rights and southern Democrats walked out of the national convention to run their own candidate, Strom Thurmond of South Carolina. This occurred because Truman desegregated the army in 1948 and seemed quite sympathetic to granting citizenship rights to returning African-American veterans. Although the decided underdog, Truman ran a vigorous campaign and carried all of the western states en route to an upset victory. Truman's foreign policy initiatives had earned him considerable support in America and Republicans had underestimated his true popularity.

Origins of the Cold War

American leaders knew going into World War II that they would need the help of the Soviet Union to help win the war. By the middle of 1940 only England and Russia were free of German control in Europe. At the end of the war the Russians had suffered enormous losses (between 25-30 million killed) and its leaders, acting out of nationalistic concerns and communist ideology, were determined to control eastern and central Europe through which the Germans had attacked them. Rapid American demobilization left the U.S. with insufficient troop strength in Europe to stop Russian control of these areas and threats to America's other European allies. Beginning in 1945-46 President Truman began a strategy of political and military actions to contain Russian expansionism. One policy decision was the reintroduction of Selective Service.

United States Foreign Policy

The United States formulated a foreign policy aimed at stopping the spread of communism. This became known as the containment policy. In 1947, the United States announced aid to Greece and Turkey in order to stop a communist takeover of those countries. In addition to economic aid, the U.S. and Great Britain provided military assistance in the Greek civil war to prevent a communist takeover. This became known as the Truman Doctrine. In June 1947, the United States announced the Marshall Plan designed to aid in the economic recovery of most of the European countries.

Aid was offered to Russia but rejected. The purpose of the Marshall Plan was to help Europeans reconstruct their shattered economies and in doing so thwart the communists.

In 1948, President Truman ordered the Berlin Airlift to save the western sector of Berlin from Russian control. The Russians had cut off all road access to the city hoping that the Americans would withdraw. For the next six months West Berlin was supplied by air until the Russians backed down and removed their roadblocks. One year later, in 1949, the United States entered its first peacetime military alliance when it created the North Atlantic Treaty Organization (NATO).

NATO was the first of many regional military alliances that the United States would create as the containment policy became world-wide. American military bases ringed the Soviet Union and its allies. Military alliances became a permanent characteristic of American foreign policy.

Asia

The position of the United States in Asia was far weaker than in Europe. In 1949, the Chinese communists under the leadership of Mao Zedong won control of the country after a long civil war. The victory of the communists in China shocked the American people.

Korean War

American occupation forces had withdrawn from South Korea in 1949. On June 24, 1950, soldiers from North Korea invaded the South and the Korean War began. The United Nations condemned the invasion and urged members to help South Korea. President Truman appointed General Douglas MacArthur to aid the South Koreans. United Nations' troops pushed the North Koreans back across the border into their own territory. MacArthur ignored orders and continued pursuit of the enemy deep into North Korea bringing the Chinese communists into the war. Truman, angered by MacArthur's refusal to follow orders, removed him from command in 1951. The war turned into a stalemate and finally ended in 1953 with a negotiated truce settlement. More than 50,000 U.S. soldiers died in combat. The Korean War led to a new program of rearmament in the United States.

Chapter XVI -- The Eisenhower Administration, 1953-1961

Time Line

1953   First summit meeting with the Russians
1954   Brown v. Board of Education
          Desegregation of public schools
1956   Dwight Eisenhower reelected President
1958   Sputnik, First Russian space satellite
1959   Fidel Castro assumes power in Cuba
1960   John F. Kennedy elected President

Key Terms

Segregation
Vietminh
Communist China
I.C.B.M.

Dwight Eisenhower came to the presidency thus ending 20 years of Democratic party control of that office. He was a World War II hero, who after the war, became president of Columbia University. His strong personality enabled him both to inspire and give confidence to the country. Fondly known as 'Ike,' he sought to act as conciliator at a time when political extremists on both sides were vocal. Despite his desire to be a conciliator, Eisenhower's administration was characterized by major domestic and foreign policy challenges.

Civil Rights

The civil rights movement gained momentum after the end of World War II. A system of segregation had rooted itself particularly in the south, since the end of reconstruction. Young urban politicians like Hubert Humphrey split the Democratic party when they insisted on a civil rights plan in the party's platform in 1948. President Truman had desegregated the U.S. armed forces in 1948 and the Korean War contingent was fully integrated.

In 1954, the Supreme Court under the leadership of Chief Justice Earl Warren, ordered the public schools to be desegregated in the landmark case Brown v. Board of Education (Topeka, KS). The first test came in 1955 in

Little Rock, AK, when President Eisenhower ordered in U.S. Army troops to ensure that Central High School would be peacefully integrated.

Foreign Policy: Vietnam, China, Russia

Indo-China had been colonized by the French, until they were driven out by the Japanese in the 1930's. The French returned after World War II and faced opposition from the communist-led Vietminh under the direction of Ho Chi Minh. Vietminh forces made steady gains against the French. The French, alarmed at the possibility of losing the war, demanded United States aid in their war as a condition for France joining N.A.T.O in 1949. The French were defeated in 1954 and a truce was signed. The Vietminh gained control of North Vietnam and South Vietnam became independent. The division was supposed to be temporary, with elections scheduled in 1956 to unite the nation. The United States, however, supported the government in South Vietnam and gradually the Eisenhower administration began to send American military advisors to train the South Vietnamese army.

The American support for Nationalist China which had been ousted from the mainland in 1949 and which occupied the island of Formosa was strong. The Americans had no diplomatic relations with communist China. To try and stop possible Chinese communist expansion, the South East Asia Treaty Organization was formed (SEATO).

Changes took place in the Soviet Union after the death of Joseph Stalin in 1953. By 1955 the first 'summit meeting' between United States and the Soviet Union was held in Geneva, Switzerland. In 1956 the Hungarian uprising took place. Their attempt to oust the Russians was put down by military force. The failure of the United States to aid the Hungarians illustrated the limits of the containment policy.

Cuba and Fidel Castro

A 1959 victory in the Cuban civil war brought Fidel Castro to power. After an initial wave of support for Castro in the United States, problems between the two countries arose. Cuba nationalized American property on the island in 1960 and established friendly relations with the Russians. Eisenhower was angered by a July 1960 speech in which Castro said that the Russians would protect Cuba from American invasion with Inter-continental ballistic missiles (ICBM). Therefore, in late 1960, Eisenhower ordered the Central Intelligence agency (C.I.A.) to formulate plans to overthrow Castro.

Chapter XVII -- <u>John F. Kennedy - Lyndon Johnson, 1961-1969</u>

Time Line

1961   Bay of Pigs
1962   Cuban Missile Crisis
        University of Mississippi desegregated
1963   Assassination of John F. Kennedy
        Lyndon Johnson became President
1964   Lyndon Johnson elected President
        Civil Rights Act passed
        Gulf of Tonkin Resolution passed by Congress
1968   Tet offensive in Vietnam
        Richard Nixon elected President

Key Terms

Freedom Riders
Guerrilla warfare
Quarantine
VISTA
Federal deficit
U-2

New Frontier - Kennedy's Domestic Program

While John F. Kennedy projected an innovative, bold image in his New Frontier program (he sought to get the country 'moving again'), he really lacked the votes in Congress to get much legislation passed. This weakness was due to his slim election victory. Kennedy thus made stimulating the economy his first priority. The defense budget was increased by more than 20% in 1961 to deal with the alleged "missile gap" with the Soviet Union. The construction of 1000 multi-warhead nuclear-tipped missiles raised the U.S.-Russian defense spending to new heights. The administration also introduced an expensive effort to be first to put a man on the moon. It cost more than $25 billion for the space program. Astronaut Neil Armstrong was the first man to walk on the surface of the moon in 1969. These programs, together with a major cut in taxes, had doubled the rate of economic growth by the end of 1963. Unemployment decreased from 6% to 5% and inflation was less than 2% per year.

Civil Rights

Kennedy seemed sympathetic to Afro-American civil rights, but was not very aggressive in his support. Leaders like Dr. Martin Luther King and the Congress of Racial Equality (C.O.R.E.) put pressure on the administration. CORE arranged for buses of "freedom riders" to try and desegregate the South. As the Ku Klux Klan and other white racists savagely beat protesters in Anniston, Selma and Montgomery, Alabama, President Kennedy finally sent Federal Marshals to protect the marchers. Then, in 1962, he was forced to send soldiers onto the campus of the University of Mississippi to stop racists who were trying to halt the desegregation at that institution. In 1963, Kennedy again moved to protect civil rights marchers against the lawlessness of southern authorities. He sent in the United States Army to force the integration of the University of Alabama after Governor George Wallace had refused to obey the law.

Foreign Policy

Kennedy was a firm believer in the Containment Policy and saw the Russian government as a threat to world peace. The American nuclear arsenal tripled. The President increased the military budget overall, and formed an elite unit, the Green Berets, to fight guerrilla warfare.

Bay of Pigs

The Eisenhower plan to remove Fidel Castro was inherited by Kennedy when he took office. After a series of meetings with his advisers, Kennedy decided to go ahead with the attack in April, 1961. The attack at the Bay of Pigs was a disaster. It was poorly planned, poorly carried out, and the army of Cuban exiles was riddled with Castro's spies and was quickly routed. (For years thereafter, American agencies like the C.I.A., were engaged in an undeclared war against the Castro government, using Florida as a base of operations.) The defeat was a blow to the reputation of President Kennedy and the Russian leader Nikita Khrushchev believed Kennedy was weak and could be manipulated.

Cuban Missile Crisis

During the Summer of 1961, Fidel Castro's brother, Raul, went to Moscow and Khrushchev agreed to supply missiles to Cuba. In October 1962 American aerial photography planes (U-2) took pictures of missile silos under construction in Cuba.

Kennedy decided to quarantine or blockade Cuba to force the dismantling of the missiles already in place. A confrontation loomed between American naval vessels and Russian ships that approached the American intercept zone. The United States was placed on a war footing, thousands of combat troops were sent to Florida as a staging area, and reservists were called to active duty. When it became clear what was happening, the world feared the possibility of global nuclear warfare. On October 25, 1962, Nikita Khrushchev agreed to Kennedy's demands that the missiles be removed in return for American guarantees not to try and invade Cuba. The Americans also agreed to remove obsolete missiles that were placed in Turkey which was not made public at the time. Because of his seeming 'grace under pressure', Kennedy's popularity soared after the missile crisis ended.

Vietnam

John Kennedy expanded Eisenhower's commitment to aid South Vietnam against the communist North and began the escalation that led to America's longest and most expensive war. In 1962 more financial aid, supplies and military advisers were sent to South Vietnam. The South Vietnamese government under President Diem, our ally, resisted all calls for national reform and, with American acquiescence, Diem was overthrown and killed. Kennedy recognized the new military-controlled government, but it, too, was unresponsive to American ideas about change. By 1963, more than 16,000 American military advisers were in Vietnam and many were engaged in combat. There is still a debate as to what Kennedy planned to do by the end of 1963: whether to escalate further or gradually to end the Vietnam involvement.

The Kennedy Assassination: November 22, 1963

While campaigning in Texas, in preparation for the 1964 election campaign, John F. Kennedy was assassinated in Dallas. He was shot in an open car while riding in a motorcade. Lee Harvey Oswald was officially charged with the murder but before he could be brought to trial he was shot and killed by Jack Ruby in the Dallas police building. An official investigation was held by a commission headed by the Chief Justice of the United States, Earl Warren. The Warren Commission determined that Oswald was the lone assassin but most of the records were sealed and many questions were left unanswered. Soon after the decision of the Commission was announced, many critics challenged the report. Due to the belief that the government had lied about so many aspects of national policy, many Americans persisted in the conviction that the report was a coverup for some sort of conspiracy to kill Kennedy.

Lyndon Johnson and the Great Society

Lyndon Johnson, an experienced leader of the United States Senate from Texas, had been selected Vice President by Kennedy in 1960 and quickly assumed the powers as President. Johnson was able to push Kennedy's domestic program through Congress in part because of the national trauma over the assassination of Kennedy.

Seeking to put his own stamp on the administration, Johnson introduced 'The Great Society' slogan; it was a wide variety of laws, designed to accomplish many goals, among which was to sustain long term prosperity, fulfill the civil rights agenda, and eliminate poverty and deprivation. Income taxes were reduced 10% and the economy responded positively. The federal deficit was reduced by one third between 1964-1966. A wide-ranging Civil Rights Act was passed in 1964 and strengthened in 1965. The Equal Opportunities Employment Act (EEOC) was created. A "war on poverty" was declared and resulted in the passage of the Job Corps, VISTA and Head Start. Cumulatively, these laws were intended to end the poverty in America that engulfed about one fifth of the population, especially those people living in the great cities. However, the Great Society program would quickly be supplanted by the need to pay for the escalating war in Vietnam.

Johnson and Vietnam

The deepening involvement in Vietnam consumed Lyndon Johnson, ultimately destroyed his Presidency, and led to the widespread disillusionment with him and his administration.

In August 1964 an "alleged" clash between U.S. naval vessels and North Vietnamese ships in the South China Sea led to the passage in Congress of the Gulf of Tonkin Resolution. This gave the President the authority to escalate the war in Vietnam. Johnson had a very successful two years as President and was triumphantly reelected on his own over the Republican candidate, Senator Barry Goldwater of Arizona. Johnson ran in the 1964 campaign with the promise that he would not send American boys to fight an Asian war. He portrayed his opponent as a man capable of provoking a nuclear war with Russia. It later became known that Johnson planned a significant expansion of the ground forces in Vietnam once the election had been won.

_____ 10. The Great Society was a federal government effort to provide expanded government efforts A) To assist those most in need B) To make America stronger C) To assist Vietnam D) To help Canada and Mexico compete economically with the U.S.

Chapter XVIII -- <u>Richard M. Nixon, 1969-1977</u>

Time Line

1969   Bombing expanded into Laos and Cambodia
1972   Nixon visited China and Soviet Union
        Break-in at Democratic party headquarters - Watergate
        Richard Nixon reelected President
1973   Spiro Agnew resigned as Vice President
        Gerald Ford named Vice President
        American forces pull out of Vietnam
1974   Watergate investigation continued
        Nixon resigned from the Presidency
        Gerald Ford became President
        Nelson Rockefeller named Vice President
        Ford pardoned Richard Nixon

Key Terms

Primary election
Vietnamization
Watergate
Impeachment
CREEP
SALT
25th Amendment

Election of 1968

The turmoil of the 1960's spilled over into the presidential election campaign. In three incredible months, March through May, events shook the Democratic party. In March, Lyndon Johnson pulled out of the race. In April, Dr. Martin Luther King was shot and killed in Memphis, Tennessee. Then in May, immediately after he had won the Democratic presidential primary election in California, Robert Kennedy was assassinated. Vice President Hubert Humphrey then received the presidential nomination for the Democrats. His pro-Vietnam war stance angered many and the convention in Chicago was marked by chaotic rioting. Richard Nixon was the Republican candidate. An independent, George Wallace, Governor of Alabama, an opponent of greater civil rights for minorities, entered the race. Nixon won a very close election in which Wallace polled 14% of the popular vote.

Nixon hoped to make his mark on the presidency through his dealings in foreign policy rather than domestic affairs. Harvard Professor Henry Kissinger, later Secretary of State, became the architect of Nixon's foreign policy.

Vietnam

Nixon was elected in 1968 in part because of his pledge to bring the war to a speedy conclusion. The President, however, was preoccupied with preserving American pride and world influence. In 1969, a period of Vietnamization was begun. This involved the transfer of increased military responsibility to the South Vietnamese army and a phased reduction in the American participation. By 1972, only 30,000 American troops remained, down from 500,000. However, in 1972, it was learned that as early as 1969 Nixon had widened the bombing war by targeting Laos and Cambodia. Riots ensued and several student protesters were shot and killed by Ohio National Guardsmen on the Campus of Kent State University. Finally, on January 23, 1973, the United States pulled its remaining troops out of Vietnam. More than 58,000 American soldiers died and over 300,000 were wounded.

China

In keeping with the secretive nature of the Nixon-Kissinger foreign policy, the nation was shocked in 1971 when Nixon announced that he would visit mainland China. He went in 1972 and met with Mao Zedong and official diplomatic relations were restored in 1979. The Nixon visit seemed to end 20 years of open hostility.

The Soviet Union and Detente

Richard Nixon also made a trip to Moscow in 1972 where trade and technological agreements were signed. Strategic Arms Limitation Talks (SALT) began and two treaties to control the armament race were agreed upon. These limitations were attempts to slow the growth of nuclear armaments, reduce cold war tensions, and had the effect of boosting Nixon's reelection chances in 1972.

Election of 1972

Richard Nixon seemed assured of reelection. His success in dealing with China and Russia plus the scaling down of the war in Vietnam were considered positive achievements. His "law and order" approach to domestic problems won him considerable support. The independent candidate George Wallace was shot at a campaign rally, paralyzed from the waist down, and was forced to withdraw from the election campaign. The Democratic candidate was South Dakota Senator George McGovern. He campaigned on a peace platform and called for a withdrawal from Vietnam. In the election, Nixon carried every state but one to win a huge victory.

Watergate, Spiro Agnew and Impeachment

In his desire for every vote in 1972, Nixon left no stone unturned. His Committee to Reelect the President (C.R.E.E.P.) had engaged in a series of "dirty tricks". One of these was a plan to break in and plant listening devices (bugs) on the telephone lines of the Democratic National Party Headquarters located at the Watergate Hotel and Office Complex in Washington, D.C. An alert security guard foiled the break-in, and police arrested several people associated with CREEP (some of whom were former CIA agents).

The White House, on orders from the President, began an elaborate cover-up of the burglary which ultimately led to Nixon's resignation.

Vice President Spiro Agnew, who had gained considerable notoriety because of his attacks on administration critics, had been indicted for bribery and income tax evasion. In return for this plea of "no contest" (equal to guilty) and resignation of the Vice Presidency, Agnew was able to avoid imprisonment. Acting pursuant to the 25th Amendment, President Nixon chose Michigan Congressman Gerald Ford to be his Vice President and Congress quickly confirmed him.

Congressional investigations began soon after Nixon's triumphant inauguration. In a Senate hearing a discovery was made that President Nixon had tape recorded all Oval Office conversations. Over Nixon's objections, the Supreme Court ordered a release of the tapes. The tapes directly incriminated him in the cover-up, as early as a few days after the Watergate burglary. The nation was transfixed by the televised hearings of the House Judiciary Committee debate and adoption of an indictment

Chapter XIX -- Jimmy Carter, 1977-1981

Time Line

1976   Jimmy Carter elected President
1978   Camp David accord with Israel-Egypt
1979   Diplomatic relations formalized with China
1980   Iranian Hostage crisis
        Summer Olympic boycott
        Ronald Reagan elected President

Key Terms

Hostage Crisis
Ayatollah Khomeni
OPEC Cartel
SALT II

Election of 1976

In the Presidential primary campaign of 1976, Gerald Ford won the Republican nomination after fighting off a strong challenge from California Governor Ronald Reagan. Georgia Governor Jimmy Carter emerged from a group of Democratic candidates to win the nomination. Carter campaigned as an outsider who would restore honesty and integrity to government in Washington, D.C. A huge early lead in the polls almost evaporated, but Carter was able to hold on for a slim victory. Gerald Ford was never able to overcome the public outrage over the pardon of former President Richard Nixon.

Foreign Policy

Jimmy Carter emphasized human rights and tried to use it as a yardstick in his foreign policy. Secretary of State, Cyrus Vance, worked hard to eliminate human rights abuses in Latin America, South Africa and Asia. In addition, negotiations with Panama produced a treaty that promised to turn over the Canal and Canal Zone to Panama in 1999.

The Soviet Union

Negotiations continued with the Russians for a new treaty on strategic arms limitations (SALT II), but this policy collapsed when the Russians invaded Afghanistan. The treaty was withdrawn and Carter ordered a boycott of the 1980 Olympic games which were to be held in Moscow. In addition, Carter supported expensive new weapons systems, like the MX, a mobile nuclear-tipped missile.

Middle East

President Carter's finest achievement in foreign affairs was his part in bringing together bitter enemies, Israel and Egypt, for a peace treaty. Camp David did not, however, end the Middle East conflict between Arabs and Israelis, as Carter hoped.

Iran, Oil and the Hostage Crisis

Inflation was high when Jimmy Carter took over from Ford in 1977. However, it skyrocketed during his administration. The oil-producing nations led by Iran, doubled the price of oil to $30 a barrel. Interest rates approached 20%, near the end of Carter's term. Rising inflation and trouble with the Russians were difficult, but the real problem for Carter lay ahead with Iran.

The United States had been allied with the Shah of Iran since 1953 when the C.I.A. restored him to power after a popular revolution. He ruled with an iron hand, using secret police and torture to keep his opponents in line. In 1979, the Shah was overthrown by Islamic fundamentalists led by the Ayatollah Ruholla Khomeni. Khomeni had been exiled to France where he worked to end the rule of the Shah. Khomeni preached hatred for the United States because of it's support for the Shah's government. In 1979, mobs stormed the American embassy in Teheran and seized 53 American hostages. Thus began the Iranian hostage crisis, which lasted 444 days. This crisis alarmed, angered and embarrassed the American people and the Carter administration. It became clear that President Carter was unable to solve the problem because the Iranian government refused to release the hostages. By the end of his term, Carter's popularity had dipped below a 25% approval rating.

Chapter XX -- The Era of Ronald Reagan, 1981-1989

Time Line

1981   Reagan Administration funds Contras in Nicaragua
1983   American troops invade Grenada
1984   Ronald Reagan reelected President
1985   Mikhail Gorbachev assumes power in Russia
1986   Iran-Contra scandal

Key Terms

Reaganomics
AIDS
Deregulation

Reaganomics - The Program

Ronald Reagan promised to cut inflation, rebuild the nation's defenses and restore economic growth, while at the same time cutting the size of the Federal Government.

Reagan blamed the nation's economic problems on declining capital investment. He believed the nation's problems were caused by an outdated tax system that did not sufficiently reward risk-taking. To deal with this, he called for a tax cut that was passed by Congress in 1981. Taxes were slashed 25% between 1981-1983. In 1986 tax rates on the wealthiest Americans were reduced to 28%.

Reaganomics - The Result

The defense budget was more than doubled between 1981-1987, from $165 billion to more than $330 billion. Banking, airline and natural gas industries, among others, were deregulated. Regulatory controls were relaxed on most industrial production and development. Offshore drilling and leasing of public lands increased. Mandated automobile safety measures were delayed and the Clean Air Act was not enforced.

Ronald Reagan left office in 1989 with the country enjoying its longest post-war economic expansion. However, critics charged that this was not true prosperity but one in which only the wealthy speculators profited. The

Federal budget deficit grew from $750 billion to $3.5 trillion during Reagan's eight years in office. Deregulation spawned scandals in the banking industry (Savings and Loan Associations) and on Wall Street where speculators like Michael Milken were eventually prosecuted, jailed and fined. Many of these problems were to surface during the next administration. In addition, a major gap was growing between the rich and the middle class in the United States.

Social Problems

Reagan tried to halt the growth of social programs which he believed robbed Americans of their traditional spirit of independence and self reliance. His administration significantly reduced spending in such areas as Education, Child Nutrition, Food Stamps, and Job Training programs.

Sexually Transmitted Disease

By 1980, medical experts were uncovering the first cases of AIDS in the United States. After some study it was linked to a HIV virus. AIDS research funds were slow to come from the administration which believed that it was basically a homosexual problem, since a large percentage of cases involved gay men and lesbians. The disease was also linked to drug abusers who shared infected needles. By 1987, more than 21,000 people had died of the disease and little was done to promote research by an administration that was hostile to social services and medical research.

Foreign Policy

Cold War tensions escalated early in the administration. Reagan described the Soviet Union as an "Evil Empire" and embarked upon a wide-variety of new and expensive arms programs, especially Star Wars, a plan to develop a missile shield around the United States.

Latin America

Reagan's policy aimed to keep communist-led governments out of Latin America. In 1983, a Marxist inspired government came to power in the small Caribbean nation of Grenada. Cuban aid had been given and an airfield was under construction to use as a refueling base for Russian planes. In October American troops invaded Grenada, killed or captured 750 Cuban soldiers and placed a new, American-supported government in power.

Nicaragua ousted its long time brutal dictator, Anastasio Somoza. In 1979, a new regime, led by leftist-leaning group called the Sandinistas, was hostile to the United States took control. The new government turned to the Soviet Union for armaments. The Reagan administration then began to actively support anti-government forces called the Contras. In 1984 Congress expressed its opposition to United States involvement and ordered all aid to the Contras stopped. Defying Congressional mandates, the administration circumvented the legislation.

Finally, in 1987, a regional peace plan proposed by the President of Costa Rica, Oscar Arias Sanchez was accepted. In 1990 free elections were held and the Sandinistas were voted out of office.

The Iran-Contra Mess

The greatest scandal of the Reagan administration was the Iran-Contra affair. National Security Advisor Admiral John Poindexter and his assistant Lt. Colonel Oliver North secretly sold American arms to the Iranian government (supposedly to gain the release of American hostages held in Lebanon) and used the $12 million profit to finance the Contras in the Nicaraguan civil war. President Reagan secretly authorized this sale in January 1986, but maintained, in November 1986, when the sale became public, that he knew nothing about the diversion of funds to the Contras. Congress had specifically banned American aid to the Contras. The press, public, and congressional leaders demanded an investigation. Congress created a Joint Committee, President Reagan established a presidential board, and a special prosecutor, Lawrence Walsh, was authorized under a law passed during the Watergate scandal, to investigate what had actually happened. While these investigations took place, questions were raised about the role of Vice President George Bush, a former CIA Director, in the decisions that led to Iran-Contra, but he claimed that he had been left out of all discussions concerning these transactions. (These denials would come back to haunt him a few years later when evidence surfaced that he had in fact been at the various key meetings at which the arms sales had been decided.)

Iran-Contra caused a precipitous decline in Reagan's popularity and national influence, although most Americans wanted to believe that he really did not know what Admiral Poindexter and Lt. Col. North and a small group of former government officials were actually doing in the basement of the White House. Because North and Poindexter were given immunity to testify before the Joint Congressional Committee, the guilty verdicts in their subsequent trials were reversed on appeal. The scandal, however, reinforced the cynicism about America's government that had surfaced during the Vietnam war era and had been heightened by the Watergate scandals of the 1970's.

91

Presidential Politics

In 1984, Ronald Reagan was easily reelected President, defeating former Vice President Walter Mondale of Minnesota. For all of his administration's problems, Ronald Reagan was still a very popular man. As he was preparing to leave the presidency after an eight year term he was called the "Teflon President", since no scandal seemed to attach to him.

Reagan hoped to see the continuation of his policies and programs in the next administration. The Republican candidate was Reagan's Vice President, George Bush. The Democratic candidate was the Governor of Massachusetts, Michael Dukakis. Dukakis ran a poor campaign and was outmaneuvered by experienced Republican campaign strategists. Bush was elected by a comfortable margin. Congress, however, remained under Democratic control.

The collapse of the Savings and Loan Associations across the country brought economic policies into sharp focus. Savings and Loans had secured from Congress, early in the 1980's, the deregulation of the industry to enable them to compete more effectively with savings and commercial banks. This led to a wave of speculation by the Savings and Loans in real estate development mortgages. When land prices dramatically fell by the late 1980's, the Savings and Loan Associations and banks incurred huge losses and many went bankrupt. Federal agencies that insure bank deposits then had to bail out the banks and the Savings and Loan Associations. The cost of this project was projected at between $350-$500 billion. In order to pay for this financial disaster Bush had to break his campaign promise -- "Read my lips-no new taxes" -- and agreed to a tax increase in 1991.

Foreign Policy

George Bush considered international relations his area of expertise. His greatest successes as President were in foreign policy.

Panama

A United States invasion of Panama was Bush's first major foreign policy action. Operation Just Cause unseated the dictator, President Manuel Noriega. Noriega had voided the results of an election in 1989 that would have ousted his party from power. At the same time a grand jury in Miami, Florida indicted Noriega on charges of engaging in the illegal drug trade. A force of 10,000 soldiers was sent to arrest Noriega and help install a new government. After some initial fighting, Noriega was ousted, deported and sent to the United States to stand trial for drug trafficking. He was found guilty by an American court and sentenced to federal prison.

Collapse of Communism

On New Year's Day 1989 people took to the streets in Eastern Europe and began demonstrations that overthrew 45 years of communist rule. The speed and success of the communist collapse surprised Americans.

The collapse of communism and the Russian empire was welcomed by the United States. People believed that the Cold War had finally come to an end after almost 45 years. The first reaction was that it would end the threat global nuclear war, the almost ceaseless small wars all over the globe, and the cost of ever-more expensive weapons systems. In its place, Americans expected a "peace dividend" in the form of relaxed tensions, a shift away from the preoccupation with building weapons to dealing with long-neglected social needs, and a significant reduction in taxation. But it soon became evident that one of the reasons for the breakup of the Soviet empire was that Russia was bankrupt. Not only had the Soviet Communists system failed to produce promised economic prosperity, but the attempt to match the western military build-up during the 1980's had brought financial ruin. Recognizing these enormous problems, Mikhail Gorbachev sought to reform the Soviet system during the 1980's, but lost control of the process. The United States and its allies were soon faced with the prospect of financially supporting democracy in Russia and Eastern Europe in order to prevent them from sliding back into anarchy or a return to dictatorship. Furthermore, with the end of the Cold War, reductions were begun in American defense spending which led to worker layoffs, military base closings and economic dislocations all over the nation.

President George Bush sought to garner some of the credit for the end of the Soviet threat, but he was also held responsible for not effectively handling the economic problems and dislocations that resulted.

Iraq

The high point of the Bush Presidency was the organization of the Gulf War coalition. On August 2, 1990, 80,000 Iraqi troops invaded and occupied Kuwait. Kuwait, a small oil rich emirate in the Persian Gulf, is a major oil supplier to the west. Several days later Iraq's leader, Saddam Hussein, announced that he had annexed Kuwait.

One week later, George Bush sent 180,000 American troops to the region Then the United States organized a coalition of allied nations against Iraq and Saddam Hussein. A United Nations resolution was passed condemning the Iraqi seizure of Kuwait. Coalition troop strength rose to more than 500,000.

The Iraqi army was very strong. It was considered to be the fourth largest in the world and basically had been equipped by the Soviet Union. However, one month of allied bombing wreaked havoc on the Iraqi's. Finally, when Operation Desert Storm began its ground attack in February, 1991, under the leadership of General Norman Schwartzkopf, the war ended in just 100 hours. It was hailed as a tremendous victory for the United States-led coalition.

Kuwait leaders were restored to power. The end of the war resulted in the restoration of Kuwaiti Independence and the removal of Iraqi soldiers. However, the end of the war did not result in the removal of Saddam Hussein.

Chapter XXII--THE CLINTON YEARS, 1993-

Time Line

1993 First Israeli-Palestinian Treaty
1994 Republicans gain control of Congress
1995 Dayton Accords signed establishing peace in Bosnia
1996 Clinton reelected President

Key Terms

NAFTA and GATT
"Whitewater"
Yitzhak Rabin and Yasir Arafat
Newt Gingrich
Personal Responsibility and Work Act 1996

Background

With a great sense of popular expectation, Bill Clinton was inaugurated President in January 1993. A vigorous young politician, born after World War II, Clinton had modeled himself upon John F. Kennedy. But, as Governor of Arkansas, a small southern state, he had no experience at the national level. Americans expected Clinton to deal with the two great challenges confronting the nation in the 1990s: Achieving the "peace dividend," which Americans interpreted to mean lower taxes, a smaller, less intrusive national government, and a reduction in American responsibilities all over the globe now that the 50 year-long Cold War was over. And, also, he was expected to mitigate the impact of globalization on the American economy. Responding to newly-emerging world markets in the 1980s and 1990s, American corporations shifted factories from America to low wage areas of the third world and fired ("downsized") large numbers of white collar and blue collar workers at home. Clinton had promised in the campaign not only to continue military spending reductions, but to grow the economy, grant tax relief for the anxious middle class, "end welfare as we know it," and grant economic assistance to the republics of the former Soviet Union to encourage the growth of democracy. In addition, in his appeal to core democratic constituencies, such as working class and black voters, he campaigned to create jobs and bring about comprehensive health care reform. However, all federal government initiatives as well as economic growth were restricted by the huge national debt which had quadrupled from 750 billion dollars to *more than 5 trillion dollars* during the 12 year Reagan-Bush administrations.

Domestic Issues

The President's domestic agenda commenced with a series of missteps and blunders in the new administration's first months. Clinton's efforts to stop the ban on gay men and women serving in the military was stymied by an outcry from the military and conservatives in both political parties. A "don't ask, don't tell" policy, which no one genuinely liked, was the result of political compromise.

An investigation of banking and real estate investments in Arkansas which involved President and Mrs. Clinton from the early 1980's, became a "cause celebre" when it appeared some administration officials attempted to interfere with the Congressional probe. The "Whitewater" affair, as the matter came to be called, became the subject of a special prosecutorial investigation along with several congressional investigations.

A substantial achievement of the administration's first year, however, was approval of a budget that included tax hikes for wealthy Americans, reductions in government spending and tax credits for poor Americans. Two more significant victories occurred when Congress approved both NAFTA (North American Free Trade Act) which eliminated most trade barriers between the United States, Mexico, and Canada and GATT (General Agreement on Trade and Tariffs) which reordered global trading barriers. Both were passed, however, over strong objections by those who believed its enactment would cause the loss of millions of jobs.

But the most startling setback was Clinton's inability to win congressional approval for reform of the nation's health care system. He had appointed a task force in 1993, headed by his wife, Hillary Rodham Clinton, which proposed the largest social welfare initiative since Social Security during the New Deal of the 1930s. The plan guaranteed medical coverage to every American while promising to hold down health care costs.

Opposition emerged from insurance companies, small business groups, doctors, pharmaceutical interests, and individuals who feared Clinton's proposal would deprive them of their current health care coverage. The resulting failure in September 1994 to find ways to compromise on the plan was seen as a major defeat for the President and the Democratic party who were denounced by the Republicans as "liberals and big spenders."

As a result, in the 1994 fall elections, although only 38% of the eligible voters participated, Republicans scored major victories, taking control of both house of Congress for the first time in 40 years. The GOP's success brought Georgia Congressman Newt Gingrich into the office of Speaker of the House of Representatives and he immediately called not only for major cuts in federal spending, tax reductions, and a balanced federal budget, but for a "new American Revolution" to transform American government and society.

Foreign Policy

President Clinton's administration faced the daunting challenge of working with Russia and the republics of the former Soviet Union to gain economic viability and stability. With less defense spending at home, the new President expected the "peace dividend" would enable the U.S. to send economic assistance to Russia and her neighbors.

As a supporter of Russian President Boris Yeltsin, Clinton emphasized his approval of Russia's fledgling efforts to build a democratic state based on capitalism and a free market economy.

The Middle East

Continuing the efforts of previous administrations, the Clinton foreign policy continued the momentum of urging peace negotiations between Israel and Palestine Liberation Front. Finally, on September 13, 1993, a treaty was signed at the White House by Israeli Prime Minister Yitzhak Rabin and Palestinian leader Yasir Arafat, granting self-rule to the Palestinians in the Gaza Strip and Jericho in an exchange of land for peace.

Bosnia

As fighting erupted in the former Yugoslavia, Clinton, who had promised to intervene with United States military forces, finally opted to engage the United Nations and Europe as peacemakers. When that policy failed, he prevailed on the warring factions to come to the United States to meet at Wright Air Force Base in Dayton, Ohio in September 1995. A comprehensive peace plan was agreed to and a 60,000 NATO contingent, containing 20,000 United States troops in its ranks, was sent to Bosnia to help enforce the peace accord.

Election Year Politics

President Clinton was able to revive his popularity by defending Social Security and Medicare--very successful federal programs with extraordinary popular support--which had come under attack by the Republicans in their drive drastically to reduce government spending and government programs. When Congressional Republicans *twice* shut down the United States Government for almost a month, Americans shrank back from the "Gingrich revolution." With the 1996 presidential election fast approaching, Clinton and the Congress cooperated in overhauling the welfare system for the first time in almost 60 years, passing "The Personal Responsibility and Work Act."

The Election of 1996

The Republican party, controlled by very conservative forces, adopted a party platform that offended women, immigrants, minorities and senior citizens. This further burdened its candidate, the former Senate Majority Leader, Bob Dole of Kansas, who many Americans already regarded as too old and too unaware of the nation's needs. Independent candidate Ross Perot entered the race but was not a major factor and he was excluded from the televised debates between Clinton and Dole. Bill Clinton ran as a moderate, successfully campaigning as the protector of middle America from radical, right-wing Republicans, and won reelection, the first Democrat to do so since Franklin Roosevelt in the 1940s. But the Republicans retained their control of Congress.

DOCUMENTS

A LETTER OF CHRISTOPHER COLUMBUS REPORTING ON HIS FIRST VOYAGE, FEBRUARY 15, 1493

Sir -- Believing that you will take pleasure in hearing of the great success which our Lord has granted me in my voyage, I write you this letter, whereby you will learn how in thirty-three days time I reached the Indies with the fleet which the most illustrious King and Queen, our Sovereigns, gave to me, where I found very many islands thickly peopled, of all which I took possession without resistance, for their highnesses. I gave the name of *La Española* [Hispaniola or San Domingo]. Thither I went and followed its northern coast. . . .

Española is a wonder. Its mountains and plains, and meadows and fields, are beautiful and rich for planting and sowing, and rearing cattle of all kinds, and for building towns and villages. The harbors on the coast, and the number and size and wholesomeness of the rivers, most of them bearing gold, surpass anything that would be believed by one who had not seen them. . . . In this island there are many spices and extensive mines of gold and other metals. The inhabitants of this and of all the other islands I have found or gained intelligence of, both men and women, go as naked as they were born, with the exception that some of the women cover one part only with a single leaf of grass or with a piece of cotton, made for that purpose. They have neither iron, nor steel, nor arms, nor are they competent to use them, not that they are not well-informed and of handsome stature, but because they are timid to a surprising degree. Their only arms are reeds . . to which they fashion small sharpened sticks, and even these they dare not use; for on several occasions it has happened that I have sent ashore two or three men to some village to hold a parley, and the people have come out in countless numbers, but, as soon as they saw our men approach, would flee with such precipitation that a father would not even stop to protect his son; and this was not because any harm had been done to any of them, for, from the first, wherever I went and got speech with them, I gave them of all that I had, such as cloth and many other things, without receiving anything in return, but they are, as I have described, incurably timid. It is true that when they are reassured and have thrown off their fear, they are guileless, and so liberal of all they have that no one would believe it who had not seen it. They never refuse anything that they possess when it is asked of them; on the contrary, they offer it themselves, and they exhibit so much loving kindness that they would even give their hearts; and, whether it be something of value or of little worth that is offered to them, they are satisfied. . . . I gave away a thousand good and pretty articles which I had brought with me in order to win their affection; and that they might be led to become Christians, and be well inclined to love and serve their Highnesses and the whole Spanish nation, and that they might aid us by giving us things of which we stand in need, but which they possess in abundance.

They are not acquainted with any kind of worship, and are not idolators; but believe that all power and, indeed, all good things are in heaven, and with this belief received me at every place at which I touched, after they had overcome their apprehension. And this does not spring from ignorance, for they are very intelligent, and navigate all these seas, and relate everything to us, so that it is astonishing what a good account they are able to give of everything; but they have never seen men with clothes on, nor vessels like ours. On my reaching the Indies, I took by force, in the first island that I discovered, some of these natives, that they might learn our language and give me information in regard to what existed in these parts; and it so happened that they soon understood us and we them, either by words or signs, and they have been very serviceable to us. They are still with me, and, from repeated conversations that I have had with them, I find that they still believe that I come from heaven. And they were the first to say this wherever I went, and the others ran from house to house and to the neighboring villages, crying with a loud voice: "Come, come, and see the people from heaven!" And thus they all, men as well as women, after their minds were at rest about us, came, both large and small, and brought us something to eat and drink, which they gave us with extraordinary kindness. . . .

Finally, and speaking only of what has taken place in this voyage, which has been so hasty, their Highnesses may see that I shall give them all the gold they require, if they will give me but a very little assistance; spices also, and cotton, as much as their Highnesses shall command to be shipped; and slaves, as many as they of shall order to be shipped -- and these shall be from idolaters. . . . I think also I have found rhubarb and cinnamon, and I shall find a thousand other valuable things by means of the men that I have left behind me. . . .Much more I would have done if my vessels had been in as good a condition as by rights they ought to have been. . . .

Done on board the caravel, off the Canary Islands, on the fifteenth of February, fourteen hundred and ninety-three.

THE ADMIRAL

MAYFLOWER COMPACT
November 11, 1620

IN THE NAME OF GOD, AMEN. We, whose names are underwritten, the Loyal Subjects of our dread Sovereign Lord King *James, by the Grace of God, of Great Britain, France, and Ireland,* King, *Defender of the Faith,* &c.

Having undertaken for the Glory of God, and Advancement of the Christian Faith, and the Honour of our King and Country, a Voyage to plant the first Colony in the northern Parts of Virginia; Do by these Presents, solemnly and mutually, in the Presence of God and one another, covenant and combine ourselves together into a civil Body Politick, for our better Ordering and Preservation, and Furtherance of the Ends aforesaid: And by Virtue hereof do enact, constitute, and frame, such just and equal Laws, Ordinances, Acts, Constitutions, and Officers, from time to time, as shall be thought most meet and convenient for the general Good of the Colony; unto which we promise all due Submission and Obedience.

IN WITNESS whereof we have hereunto subscribed our names at *Cape-Cod* the eleventh of *November,* in the Reign of our Sovereign Lord King *James,* of *England, France,* and *Ireland,* the eighteenth, and of Scotland, the fifty-fourth, *Anno Domini, 1620.*

WILLIAM BRADFORD OF PLYMOUTH PLANTATION ON PEQUOT WAR
1637

In the year 1634, the Pequents (a stoute and warlike people), who had made warrs with sundry of their neighbours, and puft up with many victories, grue now at varience with the Narigansets, a great people bordering upon them. The Narigansets held correspondance and termes of friendship with the English of the Massachusetts.

In the forepart of this year, (1637) the Pequents fell openly upon the English at Conightecute, in the lower parts of the river, and slew sundry of them, (as they were at work in the fields,) both men and women, to the great terrour of the rest; and wente away in great pride and triumph, with many high threats. They allso assalted a fort at the rivers mouth, though strong and well defended; and though they did not their prevails, yet it struk them with much fear and astonishmente to see their bould attempts in the face of danger; which made them in all places to stand upon their gard, and to prepare for resistance, and ernestly to solissite their friends and confederats in the Bay of Massachusets to send them speedy aide, for they looked for more forcible assaults.

In the mean time, the Pequents, espetially in the winter before, sought to make peace with the Narigansets, and used very pernicious arguments to move them therunto: as that the English were stranegers and begane to overspred their contrie, and would deprive them therof in time, if they were suffered to grow and increase; and if the Narigansets did assist the English to subdue them, they did but make way for their owne overthrow for if they were rooted out, the English would soone take occasion to subjugate them; and if they would harken to them, they should not neede to fear the strength of the English:

But againe when they considered how much wrong they had received from the Pequents, and what an oppertunitie they now had by the help of the English to right them selves, revenge was so sweete unto them, as it prevailed about all the rest; so as they resolved to joyne with the English againsts them, and did. The Court here agreed forwith to send 50 men at their own charg;

So they sent on, and so ordered their march, as the Indeans brought them to a forte of the enimies (in which most of their cheefe men were) before day. They approached the same with great silence, and surrounded it both with English and Indeans, that they might not breake out; and so assualted them with great courage, shooting amongst them, and entered the forte with all speed; and those that first entered found sharp resistance from the enemie, who both shott at and grapled with them; others rane into their howses, and brought out fire, and sett them on fire, which soone tooke in their matts, and, standing close togeather, with the wind, all was quickly on a flame, and therby more were burnte to death than was otherwise slain;

It was conceived they thus destroyed about 400 at this time. It was a fearfull sight to see them thus frying in the fyer, and the streams of blood quenching the same, and horrible was the stinck and sente there of; but the victory had wrought so wonderfuly for them.

The Narigansett Indeans, all this while, stood round aboute, but aloofe from all danger, and left the whole execution to the English, except it were the stoping of any that broke away, insulting over their enimies in this their ruine and miserie, when they saw them dancing in the flames, calling them by a word in their owne language, signifing. O brave Pequents!

FUNDAMENTAL ORDERS OF CONNECTICUT
January 14, 1639

Forasmuch as it hath pleased the Allmighty God by the wise dispositon of his divyne pruvidence so to Order and dispose of things that we The Inhabitants and Residents of Windsor, Harteford and Wethersfield are now cohabiting and dwelling in and uppon the River of Conectecotte and the Lands thereunto adioyneing; And well knowing where a peope are gathered togather the word of God requies that to mayntayne the peace and union of such a people there should be an orderly and decent Government established according to God, to order and dispose of the affayres of the people at all seasons as occation shall require; doe assotiate and conioyne our selves to be as one Publike State or Commonwelth; and doe, for our selves and our Successors and such as shall be adioyned to us att any tyme hereafter, enter into Combination and Confederation togather, to mayntayne and presearve the liberty and purity of the gospell of our Lord Jesus which we now professe, as also the disciplyne of the Churches, which according to the truth of the said gospell is now practised amongst us; As also in our Civell Affaires to be guided and governed according to such Lawes, Rules, Orders and decrees as shall be made, ordered & decreed, as followeth: --

It is Ordered . . . that there shall be yerely two generall Assemblies or Courts, the one the second thursday in Aprill, the other the second thursday in September, folloiwng; the first shall be called the Courte of Election, wherein shall be yerely Chosen . . . soe many Magestrats and other publike Officer as shall be found requisitte: Whereof one to be chosen Governour for the yeare ensuing and untill another be chosen, and noe other Magestrate to be chosen for more than one yeare; provided allwayes there be sixe chosen besids the Governour; which being chosen and sworne according to an Oath recorded for that purpose shall have power to administer justice according to the Lawes here established.

It is Ordered . . . that noe person be chosen Governor above once in two yeares, and that the Governor be alwayes a member of some approved congregation, and formerly of the Magestracy within this Jurisdiction;

It is Ordered . . . that to the aforesaid Courte of Election the severall Townes shall send their deputyes, and when the Elections are ended they may proceed in any publike searvice as at other Courts. Also the other Generall Courte in September shall be for makeing of lawes, and any other publike occation, which conserns the good of the Commonwelth.

SELECTIONS FROM CONNECTICUT'S EARLY LAWS
1650

Forasmuch as the free fruition of such liberties, immunities, privileges as humanity, civility and Christianity call for, as due to every man in his place and proportion, without impeachment and infringement, has ever been and ever will be the tranquility and stability of churches and commonwealths; and the denial or deprival thereof, the disturbance, if not ruin of both: It is thereof ordered by this Court, and authority thereof, that no man's life shall be taken away; no man's honor or good name shall be stained; no man's person shall be arrested, restrained, banished, dismembered, nor any way punished; no man shall be deprived of his wife or children; no man's goods or estates shall be taken away from him nor anyways damaged, under color of law, or countenance of authority; unless it be by the virtue or equity of some express law of the country warranting the same, established by a General Court and sufficiently published, or in case of the defect of a law, in any particular case, by the Word of God.

Capital Laws

1. If any man after legal conviction shall have or worship any other God but the Lord God, he shall be put to death. Deut. 13:6, 17:2, Ex. 22:20.

2. If any man or woman be a witch, that is, has or consults with a familiar spirit, they shall be put to death. Ex. 22: 18; Lev. 20:27; Deut. 18:10, 11.

3. If any person shall blasphemy the name of God the Father, Son or Holy Ghost with direct, express, presumptuous, or high-handed blasphemy, or shall curse in the like manner, he shall be put to death.

4. If any person shall commit any willful murder, which is manslaughter, committed upon malice, hatred, or cruelty, not in a man's necessary and just defense, nor by mere casualty against his will, he shall be put to death. Ex. 21: 12-14; Num. 35: 30, 31.

5. If any person shall slay another through guile, either by poisoning or other such devilish practice, he shall be put to death. Ex. 21:14.

6. If any man or woman shall lie with any beast or brute creature, by carnal copulation, they shall surely be put to death, and the beast shall be slain and buried. Lev. 20:15, 16.

7. If any man lies with mankind as he lies with woman, both of them have committed abomination, they both shall surely be put to death. Lev. 20:10, 18:20; Deut. 22:23, 24.

8. If any person commits adultery with a married or espoused wife, the adulterer and the adulteress shall surely be put to death. Lev. 20:10, 18:20; Deut. 22:23, 24.

9. If any man shall forcibly, and without consent, ravish any maid or woman that is lawfully married or contracted, he shall be put to death. Deut. 22:25.

10. If any man steals a man or mankind, he shall be put to death. Ex. 21:16.

11. If any man rise up by false witness, wittingly and of purpose to take away any man's life, he shall be put to death. Deut. 19:16, 18, 19.

12. If any man shall conspire or attempt any invasion, insurrection, or rebellion against the Commonwealth, he shall be put to death.

13. If any child or children above sixteen years old and of sufficient understanding shall curse or smite their natural father or mother, he or they shall be put to death; unless it can be sufficiently testified that the parents have been very unchristianly negligent in the education of such children, or so provoke them by extreme and cruel correction that they have been forced thereunto to preserve themselves from death maiming. Ex. 21:15, 17; Lev. 20.

14. If any man have a stubborn and rebellious son of sufficient years and understanding, viz., sixteen years of age, which will not obey the voice of his father or the voice of his mother, and that when they have chastened him will not hearken unto them, then may his father and mother, being his natural parents, lay hold on him and bring him to the magistrates assembled in Court, and testify unto them that their son is stubborn and rebellious and will not obey their voice, and chastisement, but lives in sundry notorious crimes, such a son shall be put to death. Deut. 21:20, 21. . . .

Children

The selectmen of every town in the several precincts and quarters where they dwell shall have a vigilant eye over their brethren and neighbors, to see, first, that none of them shall suffer so much barbarism in any of their families, as not to endeavor to teach by themselves or others their children and apprentices so much learning as may enable them perfectly to read the English tongue, and knowledge of the capital laws, upon penalty of 20s. for such neglect therein. Also, that all masters of families do, once a week, at least, catecize their children and servants in the grounds and principles of religion.

And further, that all parents and masters do breed and bring up their children and apprentices in some honest, lawful calling, labor, or employment, either in husbandry or some other trade profitable for themselves and Commonwealth, if they will not nor cannot train them up in learning, to fit them for higher employments.

Cruelty

It is ordered by this Court, and authority thereof, that no man shall exercise any tyranny or cruelty toward any brute creatures, which are usually kept for the use of man.

Every person shall duly resort and attend thereunto respectively upon the Lord's Day, and upon such public fast days and days of thanksgiving as are to be generally kept by the appointment of authority. And if any person within this jurisdiction shall, without just and necessary cause, withdraw himself from hearing the public ministry of the Word, after due means of conviction used, he shall forfeit for his absence, from every such public meeting, 5s. all such offenses to be heard and determined by any one magistrate, or more, from time to time.

Gaming

Upon complaint of great disorder, by the use of the game called shuffleboard, in houses of common entertainment, whereby much precious time is spent unfruitfully, and much waste of wine and beer occasioned; It is therefore ordered and enacted by the authority of this Court, that no person shall henceforth use the said game of shuffleboard in any such house, nor in any other house used as common for such purpose, upon pain for every keeper of such house to forfeit for every such offence 20s.; and for every person playing at the said game in any such house, to forfeit for every such offense 5s.; the like penalty shall be for playing in any place at any unlawful game. . . .

RESOLUTIONS OF THE STAMP ACT CONGRESS IN NEW YORK CITY
October 19, 1765

Twenty-eight delegates from nine colonies were present: Virginia, New Hampshire, North Carolina and Georgia did not send delegates.

THE members of this Congress, sincerely devoted with the warmest sentiments of affection and duty to His Majesty's person and Government, esteem it our indispensable duty to make the following declarations of our humble opinion respecting the most essential rights and liberties of the colonists, and of the grievances under which they labour, by reason of several late Acts of Parliament.

I. That His Majesty's subjects in these colonies owe the same allegiance to the Crown of Great Britain that is owing from his subjects born within the realm, and all due subordination to that august body the Parliament of Great Britain.

II. That His Majesty's liege subjects in these colonies are intitled to all the inherent rights and liberties of his natural born subjects within the kingdom of Great Britain.

III. That it is inseparably essential to the freedom of a people, and the undoubted right of Englishmen, that no taxes be imposed on them but with their own consent, given personally or by their representatives.

IV. That the people of these colonies are not, and from their local circumstances cannot be, represented in the House of Commons in Great Britain.

V. That the only representatives of the people of these colonies are persons chosen therein by themselves, and that no taxes ever have been, or can be constitutionally imposed on them, but by their respective legislatures.

VI. That all supplies to the Crown being free gifts of the people, it is unreasonable and inconsistent with the principles and spirit of the British Constitution, for the people of Great Britain to grant to His Majesty he property of the colonists.

VII. That trial by jury is the inherent and invaluable right of every British subject in these colonies.

XIII. That it is the right of the British subjects in these colonies to petition the King or either House of Parliament.

Lastly, That it is the indispensable duty of these colonies to the best of sovereigns, to the mother country, to procure the repeal of the Act for granting and applying certain stamp duties.

BENJAMIN FRANKLIN RESPONDS TO HOUSE OF COMMONS, 1766

In January 1766 Parliament conducted an investigation of the economic effects of the various laws and measures it had adopted since 1763. Franklin, was in London as agent for Pennsylvania and several other colonies. On February 13, 1766 he was called before the House of Commons for examination:

Q.   What is your name, and place of abode?

A.   Franklin, of Philadelphia.

Q.   Do the Americans pay any considerable taxes among themselves?

A.   Certainly many, and very heavy taxes.

Q.   What are the present taxes in Pennsylvania, laid by the laws of the Colony?

A.   There are taxes on all estates real and personal, a poll tax, a tax on all offices, professions, trades and businesses, according to their profit; an excise upon all wine, rum and other spirits; and a duty of ten pounds per head on all Negroes imported, with some other duties. . . .

Q.   Are not the Colonies, from their circumstances, very able to pay the stamp duty?

A.   In my opinion, there is not gold and silver enough in the Colonies to pay the stamp duty for one year.

Q.   Don't you know that the money arising from the stamps was all to be laid out in America?

A.   I know it was appropriated by the act to the American service; but it will be spent in the conquered Colonies, where the soldiers are, not in the Colonies that pay it.

Q.   Is there not a balance of trade due from the colonies where the troops are posted , that will bring back the money to the old Colonies?

A. I think not. I believe very little would come back. I know of no trade likely to bring it back. I think it would come from the Colonies where it was spent directly to England; for I have always observed, that in every colony the more plenty the means of remittance to England the more goods are sent for, and the more trade with England carried on. . . .

Q. How many white men do you suppose there are in North America?

A. Abut 300,000 from sixteen to sixty years of age.

Q. What may be the amount of one year's imports into Pennsylvania from Britain?

A. I have been informed that our merchants compute the imports from Britain to be above 500,000 pounds.

Q. What may be the amount of the produce your province exported to Britain?

A. It must be small, as we produce little that is wanted in Britain. I suppose it cannot exceed 40,000 pounds.

Q. How then do you pay the balance?

A. The balance is paid by the produce carried to the West Indies, and sold in our own islands, or to the French, Spaniards, Danes and Dutch; by the same carried to other colonies in North America, as to New England, Nova Scotia, Newfoundland, Carolina and Georgia; by the same carried to different parts of Europe, as Spain, Portugal and Italy: In all which places we receive either money, bills of exchange, or commodities that suit for remittance to Britain; which, together with all the profits on the industry of our merchants and mariners, arising in these circuitous voyages, and the freights made by their ships, center finally in Britain, to discharge the balance, and pay for British manufactures continually used in the province, or sold to foreigners by our traders.

Q. Have you heard of any difficulties lately laid on the Spanish trade?

A. Yes, I have heard that it has been greatly obstructed by some new regulations, and by the English men-of-war and cutters stationed along the coast of America.

Q. Do you think it right America should be protected by this country, and pay no part of the expense?

A. That is not the case. The colonies raised, clothed and paid, during the last war, near 25,000 men, and spent many millions.

Q. Were you not reimbursed by Parliament?

A. We were reimbursed what, in your opinion, we had advanced beyond our proportion, or beyond what might be reasonably expected from us; and it was a very small part of what we spent. Pennsylvania, in particular, disbursed about 500,000 pounds, and the reimbursements, in the whole, did not exceed 60,000 pounds.

Q. Do you not think the people of America would submit to pay the stamp duty, if it was moderated?

A. No, never, unless compelled by force of arms. . . .

Q. What was the temper of America towards Great Britain before the year 1763?

A. The best in the world. They submitted willingly to the government of the Crown, and paid, in all their courts, obedience to acts of Parliament. Numerous as the people are in the several old provinces, they cost you nothing in forts, citadels, garrisons or armies, to keep them in subjection. They were governed by this country at the expense only of a little pen, ink and paper. They were led by a thread. They had not only a respect, but an affection, for Great Britain, for its laws, its customs and manners, and even a fondness for its fashions, that greatly increased the commerce. Natives of Britain were always treated with particular regard; to be an Old England man, was, of itself, a character of some respect, and gave a kind of rank among us.

Q. And what is their temper now?

A. O, very much altered.

Q. Did you ever hear the authority of Parliament to make laws for America questioned till lately?

A. The authority of Parliament was allowed to be valid in all laws, except such as should lay internal taxes. It was never disputed in laying duties to regulate commerce. . . .

Q. In what light did the people of America use to consider the Parliament of Great Britain?

A. They considered the Parliament as the great bulwark and security of their liberties and privileges, and always spoke of it with the utmost respect and veneration: arbitrary ministers, they thought, might possibly, at times, attempt to oppress them, but they relied on it, that the Parliament, on application, would always give redress. They remembered, with gratitude, a strong instance of this, when a bill was brought into Parliament, with a clause to make royal instructions laws in the colonies, which the House of Commons would not pass, and it was thrown out.

Q. And have they not still the same respect for Parliament?

A. No, it is greatly lessened.

Q. To what cause is that owing?

A. To a concurrence of causes; the restraints lately laid on their trade, by which the bringing of foreign gold and silver into the colonies was prevented; the prohibition of making paper money among themselves; and then demanding a new and heavy tax by stamps; taking away at the same time, trial by juries, and refusing to receive and hear their humble petitions.

Q. Don't you think they would submit the Stamp Act, if it was modified, the obnoxious parts taken out, and the duties reduced to some particulars, of small moment?

A. No, they will never submit to it. . . .

Q. Was it an opinion in America before 1764, that the Parliament had no right to lay taxes and duties there?

A. I never heard any objection to the right of laying duties to regulate commerce; but a right to lay internal taxes was never supposed to be in Parliament, as we are not represented there. . . .

Q. Would the repeal of the Stamp Act be any discouragement of your manufactures? Will the people that have begun the manufacture decline it?

A. Yes, I think they will; especially, if, at the same time, the trade is opened again, so that remittances can be easily made. I have known several instances that make it probable. In the war before last, tobacco being low, and making little remittance, the people of Virginia went generally into family manufactures. Afterwards, when tobacco bore a better price, they returned to the use of British manufactures. So fulling mills were very much disused in the last war in Pennsylvania, because bills were then plenty, and remittance could easily be made to Britain for English cloth and other goods.

Q. If the Stamp Act should be repealed, would it induce the assemblies of America to acknowledge the right of Parliament to tax them, and would they erase their resolutions?

A. No, never.

Q. Is there no means of obliging them to erase those resolutions?

A. None that I know of; they will never do it unless compelled by force of arms.

Q. Is there no power on earth that can force them to erase them?

A. No power, how great soever, can force men to change their opinions. . . .

Q. Would it be most for the interest of Great Britain, to employ the hands of Virginia in tobacco, or in manufactures?

A. In tobacco to be sure.

Q. What used to be the pride of the Americans?

A. To indulge in the fashions and manufactures of Great Britain.

Q. What is now their pride?

A. To wear their old clothes over again, till they can make new ones.

Guide To Reading Documents In This Collection

By this time you have worked your way through several documents dealing with the American colonial era.

Ask yourself as you read, what is the basic point being made in the specific document, what is the purpose of the statement, and how is that point developed and supported? How does the position in a particular document help illuminate the period or issue under review?

For example, what is the basic point being made by the colonists at the Stamp Act Congress about representation? Did their view of colonial rights differ from that of the leaders of the empire in England? What major point did Benjamin Franklin make about taxpaying in the colonies? What other important ideas did Franklin present in his testimony before the English House of Commons?

DECLARATION OF INDEPENDENCE IN CONGRESS
JULY 4, 1776

When in the course of human events, it becomes necessary for one people to dissolve the political bonds which have connected them with another, and to assume, among the powers of the earth, the separate and equal station to which the laws of nature and of nature's God entitle them, a decent respect to the opinions of mankind requires that they should declare the causes which impel them to the separation.

We hold these truths to be self-evident: That all men are created equal; that they are endowed by their Creator with certain unalienable rights; that among these are life, liberty, and the pursuit of happiness; that, to secure these rights, governments are instituted among men, deriving their just powers from the consent of the governed; that whenever any form of government becomes destructive of these ends, it is the right of the people to alter or to abolish it, and to institute new government, laying its foundation on such principles, and organizing its powers in such form, as to them shall seem most likely to effect their safety and happiness. Prudence, indeed, will dictate that governments long established should not be changed for light and transient causes; and accordingly all experience hath shown that mankind are more disposed to suffer, while evils are sufferable, than to right themselves by abolishing the forms to which they are accustomed. But when a long train of abuses and usurpations, pursuing invariably the same object, evinces a design to reduce them under absolute despotism, it is their right, it is their duty, to throw off such government, and to provide new guards for their future security. Such has been the patient sufferance of these colonies; and such is now the necessity which constrains them to alter their former systems of government. The history of the present King of Great Britain is a history of repeated injuries and usurpations, all having in direct object the establishment of an absolute tyranny over these states. To prove this, let facts be submitted to a candid world.

He has refused his assent to laws, the most wholesome and necessary for the public good.

He has forbidden his governors to pass laws of immediate and pressing importance, unless suspended in their operation till his assent should be obtained; and, when so suspended, he has utterly neglected to attend to them.

He has refused to pass other laws for the accommodation of large districts of people, unless those people would relinquish the right of representation in the legislature, a right inestimable to them, and formidable to tyrants only.

He has called together legislative bodies at places unusual, uncomfortable, and distant from the depository of their public records, for the sole purpose of fatiguing them into compliance with his measures.

He has dissolved representative houses repeatedly, for opposing, with manly firmness, his invasions on the rights of the people.

He has refused for a long time, after such dissolutions, to cause others to be elected; whereby the legislative powers, incapable of annihilation, have returned to the people at large for their exercise; the state remaining, in the mean time, exposed to all the dangers of invasions from without and convulsions within.

He has endeavored to prevent the population of these states; for that purpose obstructing the laws for naturalization of foreigners; refusing to pass others to encourage their migration hither, and raising the conditions of new appropriations of lands.

He has obstructed the administration of justice, by refusing his assent to laws for establishing judiciary powers.

He has made judges dependent on his will alone, for the tenure of their offices, and the amount and payment of their salaries.

He has created a multitude of new offices, and sent hither swarms of officers to harass our people and eat out their substance.

He has kept among us, in times of peace, standing armies, without the consent of our legislatures.

He has affected to render the military independent of, and superior to, the civil power.

He has combined with others to subject us to a jurisdiction foreign to our constitution, and unacknowledged by our laws, giving his assent to their acts of pretended legislation:

For quartering large bodies of armed troops among us;

For protecting them, by a mock trial, from punishment for any murders which they should commit on the inhabitants of these states;

For cutting off our trade with all parts of the world;

For imposing taxes on us without our consent;

For depriving us, in many cases, of the benefits of trial by jury;

For transporting us beyond seas, to be tried for pretended offenses;

For abolishing the free system of English laws in a neighboring province, establishing therein an arbitrary government, and enlarging its boundaries, so as to render it at once an example and fit instrument for introducing the same absolute rule into these colonies;

For taking away our charters, abolishing our most valuable laws, and altering fundamentally the forms of our governments;

For suspending our own legislatures, and declaring themselves invested with power to legislate for us in all cases whatsoever.

He has abdicated government here, by declaring us out of his protection and waging war against us.

He has plundered our seas, ravaged our coasts, burned our towns, and destroyed the lives of our people.

He is at this time transporting large armies of foreign mercenaries to complete the works of death, desolation, and tyranny already begun with circumstances of cruelty and perfidy scarcely paralleled in the most barbarous ages, and totally unworthy the head of a civilized nation.

He has constrained our fellow-citizens, taken captive on the high seas, to bear arms against their country, to become the executioners of their friends and brethren, or to fall themselves by their hands.

He has excited domestic insurrection among us, and has endeavored to bring on the inhabitants of our frontiers the merciless Indian savages, whose known rule of warfare is an undistinguished destruction of all ages, sexes, and conditions.

In every stage of these oppressions we have petitioned for redress in the most humble terms; our repeated petitions have been answered only by repeated injury. A prince, whose character is thus marked by every act which may define a tyrant, is unfit to be the ruler of free people.

Nor have we been wanting in our attentions to our British brethren. We have warned them, from time to time, of attempts by their legislature to extend an unwarrantable jurisdiction over us. We have reminded them of the circumstances of our emigration and settlement here. We have appealed to their native justice and magnanimity; and we have conjured them, by the ties of our common kindred, to disavow these usurpations, which would inevitably interrupt our connections and correspondence. They, too, have been deaf to the voice of justice and of consanguinity. We must, therefore, acquiesce in

We, therefore, the representatives of the United States of America, in General Congress assembled, appealing to the Supreme Judge of the world for the rectitude of our intentions, do, in the name and by the authority of the good people of these colonies, solemnly publish and declare, that these United colonies are, and of right ought to be, FREE AND INDEPENDENT STATES; that they are absolved from all allegiance to the British crown, and that all political connection between them and the state of Great Britain is, and ought to be, totally dissolved; and that, as free and independent states, they have full power to levy war, conclude peace, contract alliances, establish commerce, and do all other acts and things which independent states may of right do. And for the support of this declaration, with a firm reliance on the protection of Divine Providence, we mutually pledge to each other our lives, our fortunes, and our sacred honor.

Art. I. The Stile of this confederacy shall be "The United States of America."

Art. II. Each state retains its sovereignty, freedom and independence, and every Power, Jurisdiction and right, which is not by this confederation expressly delegated to the United States, in Congress assembled.

Art. III. The said states hereby severally enter into a firm league of friendship with each other, for their common defence, the security of their liberties, and their mutual and general welfare.

Art. V. For the more convenient management of the general interests of the united states, delegates shall be annually appointed in such manner as the legislature of each state shall direct, to meet in Congress on the first Monday in November, in every year, with a power reserved to each state, to recall its delegates, or any of them, at any time within the year, and to send others in their stead, for the remainder of the Year.

In determining questions in the united states, in Congress assembled, each state shall have one vote.

Art. VI. No state shall lay any imposts or duties which may interfere with any stipulation in treaties, entered into by the united states in congress assembled, with any king, prince or state, in pursuance of any treaties already proposed by congress, to the courts of France and Spain.

No state shall engage in any war without the consent of the united states in congress assembled.

Art. IX. The united states in congress assembled, shall have the sole and exclusive right and power of determining on peace and war, except in the cases mentioned in the sixth article.

The united states in congress assembled shall also be the last resort on appeal in all disputes and differences now subsisting or that hereafter may arise between two or more states concerning boundary, jurisdiction or any other cause whatever.

Art. X. The committee of the states, or any nine of them, shall be authorised to execute, in the recess of congress, such of the powers of congress as the united states in congress assembled, by the consent of nine states, shall from time to time think expedient to vest them with; provided that

124

Art. XII. All bills of credit emitted, monies borrowed and debts contracted by, or under the authority of congress, before the assembling of the united states, in pursuance of the present confederation, shall be deemed and considered as a charge against the united states, for payment and satisfaction whereof the said united states, and the public faith are hereby solemnly pledged.

Art. XIII. Every state shall abide by the determinations of the united states in congress assembled, on all questions which by this confederation are submitted to them. And the Articles of this confederation shall be inviolably observed by every state, and the union shall be perpetual; nor shall any alteration at any time hereafter be made in any of them; unless such alteration be agreed to in a congress of the united states, and be afterwards confirmed by the legislatures of every state.

An Ordinance for the Government of the Territory of the United States northwest of the River Ohio

That there shall be appointed from time to time by Congress, ... a governor, [and] a secretary, whose commission shall continue in force for four year unless sooner revoked; he shall reside in the district, and have a freehold estate therein in 500 acres of land, while in the exercise of his office. It shall be his duty to keep and preserve the acts and laws passed by the legislature, and the public records of the district, and the proceedings of the governor in his executive department, and transmit authentic copies of such acts and proceedings, every six months, to the Secretary of Congress: There shall also be appointed a court to consist of three judges, any two of whom to form a court, who shall have a common law jurisdiction, and reside in the district, and have each therein a freehold estate in 500 acres of land while in the exercise of their offices; and their commissions shall continue in force during good behavior.

The governor and judges, or a majority of them, shall adopt and publish in the district such laws of the original States, criminal and civil, as may be necessary and best suited to the circumstances of the district, and report them to Congress from time to time which laws shall be in force in the district until the organization of the General Assembly therein, unless disapproved of by Congress; but afterwards the Legislature shall have authority to alter them as they shall think fit.

The governor, for the time being, shall be commander-in-chief of the militia, appoint and commission all officers in the same below the rank of general officers; all general officers shall be appointed and commissioned by Congress.

...The governor shall appoint such magistrates and other civil officers.... as he shall find necessary for the preservation of the peace and good order.

So soon as there shall be five thousand free male inhabitants of full age in the district, upon giving proof thereof to the governor, they shall receive authority, with time and place, to elect representatives from their countries or townships to represent them in the general assembly: *Provided*, That for every five hundred free male inhabitants, there shall be one representative, and so on progressively with the number of free male inhabitants shall the right of representation increase, until the number of representatives shall amount to twenty-five; after which, the number and proportion of representatives shall be regulated by the legislature: *Provided*, That no person be eligible or qualified to act as a representative unless he shall have been a citizen of one of the United States three years, and be a resident in

126

acres of land within the same. *Provided, also,* That a free hold in fifty acres of land in the district, having been a citizen of one of the states, and being resident in the district, or the like freehold and two years residence in the district, shall be necessary to qualify a man as an elector of a representative.

ART. 1. No person, demeaning himself in a peaceable and orderly manner, shall ever be molested on account of his mode of worship or religious sentiments, in the said territory.

ART. 3. Religion, morality, and knowledge, being necessary to good government and the happiness of mankind, schools and the means of education shall forever be encouraged. The utmost good faith shall always be observed towards the Indians; their lands and property shall never be taken from them without their consent; and, in their property, rights, and liberty, they shall never be invaded or disturbed, unless in just and lawful war authorized by Congress; but laws founded in justice and humanity, shall from time to time be made for preventing wrongs being done to them, and for preserving peace and friendship with them.

ART. 5. There shall be formed in the said territory, not less than three nor more than five States; ...And, whenever any of the said States shall have sixty thousand free inhabitants therein, such State shall be admitted, by its delegates, into the Congress of the United States, on an equal footing with the original States in all respects whatever, and shall be at liberty to form a permanent constitution and State government.

ART. 6. There shall be neither slavery nor involuntary servitude in the said territory, otherwise than in the punishment of crimes whereof the party shall have been duly convicted.

PREAMBLE

We the People of the United States, in Order to form a more perfect Union, establish Justice, insure domestic Tranquillity, provide for the common defense, promote the general Welfare, and secure the Blessings of Liberty to ourselves and our Posterity, do ordain and establish this Constitution for the United States of America.

ARTICLE I

Section 1. All legislative Powers herein granted shall be vested in a Congress of the United States, which shall consist of a Senate and a House of Representatives.

Section 2. 1. The House of Representatives shall be composed of Members chosen every second Year by the People of the several States, and the Electors in each State shall have the Qualifications requisite for Electors of the most numerous Branch of the State Legislature.

2. No Person shall be a Representative who shall not have attained to the Age of twenty-five Years, and been seven Years a Citizen of the United States, and who shall not, when elected, be an Inhabitant of that State in which he shall be chosen.

3. Representatives and direct Taxes shall be apportioned among the several States which may be included within this Union, according to their respective Numbers, which shall be determined by adding to the whole Number of free Persons, including those bound to Service for a Term of Years, and excluding Indians not taxed, three fifths of all other Persons.[1] The actual Enumeration shall be made within three Years after the first Meeting of the Congress of the United States, and within every subsequent Term of ten Years, in such Manner as they shall by Law direct. The Number of Representatives shall not exceed one for every thirty Thousand, but each State shall have at least one Representative; and until such enumeration shall be made, the State of New Hampshire shall be entitled to choose three, Massachusetts eight, Rhode-Island and Providence Plantations one, Connecticut five, New-York six, New Jersey four, Pennsylvania eight, Delaware one, Maryland six, Virginia ten, North Carolina five, South Carolina five, and Georgia three.

---

[1]Replaced by the Fourteenth Amendment.

5. The House of Representatives shall choose their Speaker and other Officers; and shall have the sole Power of Impeachment.

Section 3. 1. The Senate of the United States shall be composed of two Senators from each State, chosen by the Legislature thereof, for six Years; and each Senator shall have one Vote.[2]

2. Immediately after they shall be assembled in Consequence of the first Election, they shall be divided as equally as may be into three Classes. The Seats of the Senators of the first Class shall be vacated at the Expiration of the second Year, of the second Class at the Expiration of the fourth Year, and of the third Class at the Expiration of the sixth Year, so that one-third may be chosen every second Year; and if Vacancies happen by Resignation, or otherwise, during the Recess of the Legislature of any State, the Executive thereof may make temporary Appointments until the next Meeting of the Legislature, which shall then fill such Vacancies.[3]

3. No Person shall be a Senator who shall not have attained to the Age of thirty Years, and been nine Years a Citizen of the United States, who shall not, when elected, be an Inhabitant of that State for which he shall be chosen.

4. The Vice President of the United States shall be President of the Senate, but shall have no Vote, unless they be equally divided.

5. The Senate shall choose their other Officers, and also a President pro tempore, in the Absence of the Vice President, or when he shall exercise the Office of the President of the United States.

6. The Senate shall have the sole Power to try all Impeachments. When sitting for that Purpose, they shall be on Oath or Affirmation. When the President of the United States is tried, the Chief Justice shall preside: And no Person shall be convicted without the Concurrence of two thirds of the Members present.

7. Judgment in Cases of Impeachment shall not extend further than to removal from Office, and disqualification to hold and enjoy any Office of honor, Trust or Profit under the United States: but the Party convicted shall nevertheless be liable and subject to Indictment, Trial, Judgment and Punishment, according to Law.

---

[2]Superceded by the Seventeenth Amendment.
[3]Superceded by the Seventeenth Amendment.

Legislature thereof. But the Congress may at any time by Law make or alter such Regulation, except as to the Places of choosing senators.

2. The Congress shall assemble at least once in every Year, and such Meeting shall be on the first Monday in December, unless they shall by Law appoint a different Day.[4]

Section 5. 1. Each House shall be the Judge of the Elections, Returns and Qualifications of its own Members, and a Majority of each shall constitute a Quorum to do Business; but a smaller Number may adjourn from day to day, and may be authorized to compel the Attendance of absent Members, in such manner, and under such Penalties as each House may provide.

2. Each House may determine the Rules of its Proceedings, punish its Members for disorderly Behavior, and, with the Concurrence of two thirds, expel a Member.

3. Each House shall keep a Journal of its Proceedings, and from time to time publish the same, excepting such Parts as may in their Judgment require Secrecy; and the Yeas and Nays of the Members of either House on any question shall, at the Desire of one fifth of those Present, be entered on the Journal.

4. Neither House, during the Session of Congress, shall, without the Consent of the other, adjourn for more than three days, nor to any other Place than that in which the two Houses shall be sitting.

Section 6. 1. The Senators and Representatives shall receive a Compensation for their Services, to be ascertained by Law, and paid out of the Treasury of the United States. They shall in all Cases, except Treason, Felony and Breach of the Peace, be privileged from Arrest during their Attendance at the Session of their respective Houses, and in going to and returning from the same; and for any Speech or Debate in either House, they shall not be questioned in any other Place.

2. No Senator or Representative shall, during the Time for which he was elected, be appointed to any civil Office under the Authority of the United States, which shall have been created, or the Emoluments whereof shall have been increased during such time; and no Person holding any Office under the United States, shall be a Member of either House during his Continuance in Office.

---

[4]Changed by the Twentieth Amendment.

on other bills.

2. Every Bill which shall have passed the House of Representatives and the Senate, shall, before it become a Law, be presented to the President of the United States; If he approve he shall sign it, but if not he shall return it, with his Objections to that House in which it shall have originated, who shall enter the Objections at large on their Journal, and proceed to reconsider it. If after such Reconsideration two thirds of that House shall agree to pass the Bill, it shall be sent, together with the Objections, to the other House, by which it shall likewise be reconsidered, and if approved by two thirds of that House, it shall become a Law. But in all such Cases the Votes of both Houses shall be determined by yeas and Nays, and the Names of the Persons voting for and against the Bill shall be entered on the Journal of each House respectively. If any Bill shall not be returned by the President within ten Days (Sundays excepted) after it shall have been presented to him, the Same shall be a Law, in Manner as if he had signed it, unless the Congress by their Adjournment prevent its Return, in which Case it shall not be a Law.

3. Every Order, Resolution, or Vote to which the Concurrence of the Senate and House of Representatives may be necessary (except on a question of Adjournment) shall be presented to the President of the United States; and before the Same shall take Effect, shall be approved by him, or being disapproved by him shall be repassed by two thirds of the Senate and House of Representatives, according to the Rules and Limitations prescribed in the Case of a Bill.

Section 8. 1. The Congress shall have Power To lay and collect Taxes, Duties, Imposts and Excises, to pay the Debts and provide for the common Defence and general Welfare of the United States; but all Duties, Imposts and Excises shall be uniform throughout the United States;

2. To borrow Money on the credit of the United States;

3. To regulate Commerce with foreign Nations, and among the several States, and with the Indian Tribes;

4. To establish an uniform Rule of Naturalization, and uniform Laws on the subject of Bankruptcies throughout the United States;

5. To coin Money, regulate the Value thereof, and of foreign Coin, and fix the Standard of Weights and Measures;

6. To provide for the Punishment of counterfeiting the Securities and current Coin of the United States;

8. To promote the Progress of Science and useful Arts, by securing for limited Times to Authors and Inventors the exclusive Right to their respective Writings and Discoveries;

9. To constitute Tribunals inferior to the supreme Court;

10. To define and punish Piracies and Felonies committed on the high Seas, and Offenses against the Law of Nations;

11. To declare War, grant Letters of Marque and Reprisal, and make Rules concerning Captures on Land and Water;

12. To raise and support Armies, but no Appropriation of Money to that Use shall be for a longer Term than two Years;

13. To provide and maintain a Navy;

14. To make Rules for the government and Regulation of the land and naval Forces;

15. To provide for calling forth the Militia to execute the Laws of the Union, suppress Insurrections and repel Invasions;

16. To provide for organizing, arming, and disciplining, the Militia, and for governing such Part of them as may be employed in the Service of the United States, reserving to the States respectively, the Appointment of the Officers, and the Authority of training the Militia according to the discipline prescribed by Congress;

17. To exercise exclusive Legislation in all Cases whatsoever, over such District (not exceeding ten Miles square) as may, by Cession of particular States, and the Acceptance of Congress, become the Seat of the Government of the United States, and to exercise like Authority over all Places purchased by the consent of the Legislature of the State in which the Same shall be, for the Erection of Forts, Magazines, Arsenals, dock-Yards, and other needful Buildings; And

18. To make all Laws which shall be necessary and proper for carrying into Execution the foregoing Powers, and all other Powers vested by this Constitution in the Government of the United States, or in any Department or Officer thereof.

Section 9. 1. The Migration or Importation of such Persons as any of the States now existing shall think proper to admit, shall not be prohibited by the Congress prior to the Year one thousand eight hundred and eight, but a Tax

2. The Privilege of the Writ of Habeas Corpus shall not be suspended, unless when in Cases of Rebellion or Invasion the public Safety may require it.

3. No Bill of Attainder or ex post facto Law shall be passed.

4. No Capitation, or other direct, Tax shall be laid, unless in Proportion to the Census or Enumeration herein before directed to be taken.

5. No Tax or Duty shall be laid on Articles exported from any State.

6. No Preference shall be given by any Regulation of commerce or Revenue to the Ports of one State over those of another: nor shall Vessels bound to, or from, one State, be obliged to enter, clear, or pay Duties in another.

7. No Money shall be drawn from the Treasury, but in Consequence of Appropriations made by Law, and a regular Statement and Account of the Receipts and Expenditures of all public Money shall be published from time to time.

8. No Title of Nobility shall be granted by the United States: And no Person holding any Office of Profit or Trust under them, shall, without the Consent of the Congress, accept of any present, Emolument, Office, or Title, of any kind whatever, from any King, Prince, or foreign State.

Section 10. 1. No State shall enter into any Treaty, Alliance, or Confederation; grant Letters of Marque and Reprisal; coin Money; emit bills of Credit; make any Thing but gold and silver Coin a Tender in Payment of Debts; pass any Bill of Attainder, ex post facto Law, or Law impairing the Obligation of Contracts, or grant any Title of Nobility.

2. No State shall, without the Consent of the Congress, lay any Imposts or Duties on Imports or Exports, except what may be absolutely necessary for executing its inspection Laws; and the net Produce of all Duties and Imposts, laid by any State on Imports or Exports, shall be for the Use of the Treasury of the United States; and all such Laws shall be subject to the Revision and Control of the Congress.

3. No State shall, without the Consent of Congress, lay any Duty of Tonnage, keep Troops, or Ships of War in time of peace, enter into any Agreement or Compact with another State, or with a foreign Power, or engage in War, unless actually invaded, or in such imminent Danger as will not admit of delay.

Section 1. 1. The executive Power shall be vested in a President of the United States of America. He shall hold his Office during the Term of four Years, and, together with the Vice-President, chosen for the same Term, be elected, as follows:

2. Each State shall appoint, in such Manner as the Legislature thereof may direct, a Number of electors, equal to the whole Number of Senators and Representatives to which the State may be entitled in the Congress: but no Senator or Representative, or Person holding an Office of Trust or Profit under the United States, shall be appointed an Elector.

3. The Electors shall meet in their respective States, and vote by Ballot for two Persons, of whom one at least shall not be an Inhabitant of the same State with themselves. And they shall make a List of all the Persons voted for, and of the Number of Votes for each; which List they shall sign and certify, and transmit sealed to the Seat of the Government of the United States, directed to the President of the Senate. The President of the Senate shall, in the Presence of the Senate and House of Representatives, open all the Certificates, and the Votes shall then be counted. The Person having the greatest Number of Votes shall be the President, if such Number be a Majority of the whole Number of Electors appointed; and if there be more than one who have such Majority, and have an equal Number of Votes, then the House of Representatives shall immediately choose by Ballot one of them for President; and if no Person have a Majority, then from the five highest on the List the said House shall in like Manner choose the President. But in choosing the President, the Votes shall be taken by States, the Representation from each State having one Vote; A quorum for this Purpose shall consist of a Member or Members from two thirds of the States, and a Majority of all the States shall be necessary to a Choice. In every Case, after the Choice of the President, the Person having the greatest Number of Votes of the Electors shall be the Vice President. But if there should remain two or more who have equal Votes, the Senate shall choose from them by Ballot the Vice-President.[5]

4. The Congress may determine the Time of choosing the Electors, and the Day on which they shall give their Votes; which Day shall be the same throughout the United States.

5. No Person except a natural born Citizen, or a Citizen of the United States, at the time of the Adoption of this Constitution, shall be eligible to the Office of President; neither shall any Person be eligible to that Office who

---

[5]Modified by the Twelfth Amendment.

6. In Case of the Removal of the President from Office, or of his Death, Resignation, or Inability to discharge the Powers and Duties of the said Office, the Same shall devolve on the Vice President, and the Congress may by Law provide for the Case of Removal, Death, Resignation, or Inability, both of the President and Vice President, declaring what Officer shall then act as President, and such Officer shall act accordingly, until the Disability be removed, or a President shall be elected.[6]

7. The President shall, at stated Times, receive for his Services, a Compensation, which shall neither be increased nor diminished during the Period for which he shall have been elected, and he shall not receive within that Period any other Emolument from the United States, or any of them.

8. Before he enter on the Execution of his Office, he shall take the following Oath or Affirmation:--"I do solemnly swear (or affirm) that I will faithfully execute the Office of President of the United States, and will to the best of my Ability, preserve, protect and defend the Constitution of the United States."

Section 2. 1. The President shall be Commander in Chief of the Army and Navy of the United States, and of the Militia of the several States, when called into the actual Service of the United States; he may require the Opinion in writing, of the principal Officer in each of the executive Departments, upon any Subject relating to the Duties of their respective Offices, and he shall have Power to grant Reprieves and Pardons for Offenses against the United States, except in cases of Impeachment.

2. He shall have Power, by and with the Advice and Consent of the Senate, to make Treaties, provided two-thirds of the Senators present concur; and he shall nominate, and by and with the Advice and Consent of the Senate, shall appoint Ambassadors, other public Ministers and Consuls, Judges of the supreme Court, and all other Officers of the United States, whose Appointments are not herein otherwise provided for, and which shall be established by Law: but the Congress may by Law vest the Appointment of such inferior Officers, as they think proper, in the President alone, in the Courts of Law, or in the Heads of Departments.

3. The President shall have Power to fill up all Vacancies that may happen during the Recess of the Senate, by granting Commissions which shall expire at the End of their next Session.

---

[6]Superceded by the Twenty-fifth Amendment

as he shall judge necessary and expedient; he may, on extraordinary Occasions, convene both Houses, or either of them, and in Case of Disagreement between them, with Respect to the Time of Adjournment, he may adjourn them to such Time as he shall think proper; he shall receive Ambassadors and other public Ministers; he shall take Care that the Laws be faithfully executed, and shall Commission all the Officers of the United States.

Section 4. The President, Vice President and all civil Officers of the United States, shall be removed from Office on Impeachment for, and Conviction of, Treason, Bribery, or other high Crimes and Misdemeanors.

ARTICLE III

Section 1. The judicial Power of the United States, shall be vested in one supreme Court, and in such inferior Courts as the Congress may from time to time ordain and establish. The Judges, both of the Supreme and inferior Courts, shall hold their Offices during good Behavior, and shall, at stated Times, receive for their Services, a Compensation, which shall not be diminished during their Continuance in Office.

Section 2. 1. The judicial Power shall extend to all Cases, in Law and Equity, arising under this Constitution, the Laws of the United States, and Treaties made, or which shall be made, under their Authority;--to all Cases affecting Ambassadors, other public Ministers and Consuls;--to all Cases of admiralty and maritime Jurisdiction;--to Controversies to which the United States shall be a Party;--to Controversies between two or more States;--between a State and Citizens of another State;[7]--between Citizens of different States;--between Citizens of the same State claiming Lands under Grants of different States, and between a State, or the Citizens thereof, and foreign States, Citizens, or Subjects.

2. In all Cases affecting Ambassadors, other public Ministers and Consuls, and those in which a State shall be a Party, the supreme Court shall have original Jurisdiction. In all the other Cases before mentioned, the supreme Court shall have appellate Jurisdiction, both as to Law and Fact, with such Exceptions, and under such Regulations as the Congress shall make.

3. The Trial of all Crimes, except in Cases of Impeachment, shall be by Jury; and such Trial shall be held in the State where the said Crimes shall have been committed; but when not committed within any State, the trial shall be at such Place or Places as the Congress may by Law have directed.

---

[7]Changed by the Eleventh Amendment

and Comfort. No person shall be convicted of Treason unless on the Testimony of two Witnesses to the same overt Act, or on Confession in open Court.

2. The Congress shall have Power to declare the Punishment of Treason, but no Attainder of Treason shall work Corruption of Blood, or Forfeiture except during the Life of the Person attainted.

ARTICLE IV

Section 1. Full Faith and Credit shall be given in each State to the public Acts, Records, and judicial Proceedings of every other State. And the Congress may by general Laws prescribe the Manner in which such Acts, Records and Proceedings shall be proved, and the Effect thereof.

Section 2. 1. The Citizens of each State shall be entitled to all Privileges and Immunities of Citizens in the several States.

2. A Person charged in any State with Treason, Felony, or other Crime, who shall flee from Justice, and be found in another State, shall on Demand of the executive Authority of the State from which he fled, be delivered up, to be removed to the State having Jurisdiction of the Crime.

3. No Person held to Service or Labor in one State, under the Laws thereof, escaping into another, shall, in Consequence of any Law or Regulation therein, be discharged from such Service or Labor, but shall be delivered up on Claim of the Party to whom such Service or Labor may be due.

Section 3. 1. New States may be admitted by the Congress into this Union; but no new State shall be formed or erected within the Jurisdiction of any other State, nor any State be formed by the Junction of two or more States, or Parts of States, without the Consent of the Legislatures of the States concerned as well as of the Congress.

2. The Congress shall have Power to dispose of and make all needful Rules and Regulations respecting the Territory or other Property belonging to the United States; and nothing in this Constitution shall be so construed as to Prejudice any Claims of the United States, or of any particular State.

Section 4. The United States shall guarantee to every State in this Union a Republican Form of Government, and shall protect each of them against Invasion; and on Application of the Legislature, or of the Executive (when the Legislature cannot be convened) against domestic Violence.

The Congress, whenever two-thirds of both Houses shall deem it necessary, shall propose Amendments to this Constitution, or, on the Application of the Legislatures of two-thirds of the several States, shall call a Convention for proposing Amendments, which, in either Case, shall be valid, to all intents and Purposes, as Part of this Constitution, when ratified by the Legislatures of three-fourths of the several States, or by Conventions in three-fourths thereof, as the one or the other Mode of Ratification may be proposed by the Congress: Provided that no Amendment which may be made prior to the Year One thousand eight hundred and eight shall in any Manner affect the first and fourth Clauses in the Ninth Section of the first Article; and that no State, without its Consent, shall be deprived of its equal Suffrage in the Senate.

ARTICLE VI

1. All Debts contracted and Engagements entered into, before the Adoption of this Constitution, shall be as valid against the United States under this Constitution as under the Confederation.

2. This Constitution, and the Laws of the United States which shall be made in Pursuance thereof; and all Treaties made, or which shall be made, under the Authority of the United States, shall be the supreme law of the Land; and the Judges in every State shall be bound thereby, any Thing in the Constitution or Laws of any State to the Contrary notwithstanding.

3. The Senators and Representatives before mentioned, and the Members of the several State Legislatures, and all executive and judicial Officers, both of the United States and of the several States, shall be bound by Oath or Affirmation, to support this Constitution; but no religious Test shall ever be required as a Qualification to any Office or public Trust under the United States.

ARTICLE VII

The Ratification of the Conventions of nine States, shall be sufficient for the Establishment of this Constitution between the States so ratifying the Same.

Done in Convention by the Unanimous Consent of the States present the Seventeenth Day of September in the Year of our Lord one thousand seven hundred and Eighty seven and of the Independence of the United States of America the Twelfth.

In Witness whereof We have hereunto subscribed our Names.

the Several States, Pursuant to the Fifth Article of the Original Constitution.

AMENDMENT I
(First ten amendments passed by Congress, 1791)

Congress shall make no law respecting an establishment of religion, or prohibiting the free exercise thereof; or abridging the freedom of speech, or of the press; or the right of the people peaceably to assemble, and to petition the Government for a redress of grievances.

AMENDMENT II

A well regulated Militia, being necessary to the security of a free State, the right of the people to keep and bear Arms, shall not be infringed.

AMENDMENT III

No Soldier shall, in time of peace, be quartered in any house, without the consent of the Owner, nor in time of war, but in a manner to be prescribed by law.

AMENDMENT IV

The right of the people to be secure in their persons, houses, papers, and effects, against unreasonable searches and seizures, shall not be violated, and no Warrants shall issue, but upon probable cause, supported by Oath or affirmation, and particularly describing the place to be searched, and the persons or things to be seized.

AMENDMENT V

No person shall be held to answer for a capital or otherwise infamous crime, unless on a presentment or indictment of a Grand Jury, except in cases arising in the land or naval forces, or in the Militia, when in actual service in time of War or public danger; nor shall any person be subject for the same offence to be twice put in jeopardy of life or limb; nor shall be compelled in any criminal case to be a witness against himself, nor be deprived of life, liberty, or property, without due process of law; nor shall private property be taken for public use, without just compensation.

AMENDMENT VI

shall have been committed, which district shall have been previously ascertained by law, and to be informed of the nature and cause of the accusation; to be confronted with the witnesses against him; to have compulsory process for obtaining witnesses in his favor, and to have the Assistance of Counsel for his defence.

AMENDMENT VII

In suits at common law, where the value in controversy shall exceed twenty dollars, the right of trial by jury shall be preserved, and no fact tried by a jury, shall be otherwise reexamined in any Court of the United States, than according to the rules of the common law.

AMENDMENT VIII

Excessive bail shall not be required, nor excessive fines imposed, nor cruel and unusual punishments inflicted.

AMENDMENT IX

The enumeration in the Constitution, of certain rights, shall not be construed to deny or disparage others retained by the people.

AMENDMENT X

The powers not delegated to the United States by the Constitution, nor prohibited by it to the State, are reserved to the States respectively, or to the people.

AMENDMENT XI
(1798)

The Judicial power of the United States shall not be construed to extend to any suit in law or equity, commenced or prosecuted against one of the United States by Citizens of another State, or by Citizens or Subjects of any Foreign State.

AMENDMENT XII
(1804)

The Electors shall meet in their respective States and vote by ballot for President and Vice-President, one of whom, at least, shall not be an inhabitant of the same State with themselves; they shall name in their ballots

as President, and of all persons voted for as Vice-President, and of the number of votes for each, which lists they shall sign and certify, and transmit sealed to the seat of the government of the United States, directed to the President of the Senate;--the President of the Senate shall, in the presence of the Senate and the House of Representatives, open all the certificates and the votes shall then be counted;--The person having the greatest number of votes for President, shall be the President, if such number be a majority of the whole number of Electors appointed; and if no person have such a majority, then from the persons having the highest numbers not exceeding three on the list of those voted for as President, the House of Representatives shall choose immediately, by ballot, the President. But in choosing the President, the votes shall be taken by states, the representation from each state having one vote; a quorum for this purpose shall consist of a member or members from two-thirds of the states, and a majority of all the states shall be necessary to a choice. And if the House of Representatives shall not choose a President whenever the right of choice shall devolve upon them, before the fourth day of March next following, then the Vice-President shall act as President, as in case of the death or other constitutional disability of the President. The person having the greatest number of votes as Vice-President, shall be the Vice President, if such number be a majority of the whole number of Electors appointed, and if no person have a majority, then from the two highest numbers on the list, the Senate shall choose the Vice-President; a quorum for the purpose shall consist of two-thirds of the whole number of Senators, a majority of the whole number shall be necessary to a choice. But no person constitutionally ineligible to the office of President shall be eligible to that of Vice-President of the United States.

AMENDMENT XIII
(1865)

Section 1. Neither slavery nor involuntary servitude, except as a punishment for crime whereof the party shall have been duly convicted, shall exist within the United States, or any place subject to their jurisdiction.

Section 2. Congress shall have power to enforce this article by appropriate legislation.

AMENDMENT XIV
(1868)

Section 1. All persons born or naturalized in the United States, and subject to the jurisdiction thereof, are citizens of the United States and of the State wherein they reside. No State shall make or enforce any law which shall abridge the privileges or immunities of citizens of the United States; nor shall any State deprive any person of life, liberty, or property, without due

Section 2. Representatives shall be apportioned among the several States according to their respective numbers, counting the whole number of persons in each State, excluding Indians not taxed. But when the right to vote at any election for the choice of electors for President and Vice-President of the United States, Representatives in Congress, the Executive and Judicial officers of a State, or the members of the Legislature thereof, is denied to any of the male inhabitants of such State, being twenty-one years of age, and citizens of the United States, or in any way abridged, except for participation in rebellion, or other crime, the basis of representation therein shall be reduced in the proportion which the number of such male citizens shall bear to the whole number of male citizens twenty-one years of age in such State.

Section 3. No person shall be a Senator or Representative in Congress, or elector of President and Vice-President, or hold any office, civil or military, under the United States, or under any State, who, having previously taken an oath, as a member of Congress, or as an officer of the United States, or as a member of any State legislature, or as an executive or judicial officer of any State, to support the Constitution of the United States, shall have engaged in insurrection or rebellion against the same, or given aid or comfort to the enemies thereof. But Congress may by a vote of two-thirds of each House, remove such disability.

Section 4. The validity of the public debt of the United States, authorized by law, including debts incurred for payment of pensions and bounties for services in suppressing insurrection or rebellion, shall not be questioned. But neither the United States nor any State shall assume or pay any debt or obligation incurred in aid of insurrection or rebellion against the United States, or any claim for the loss or emancipation of any slave; but all such debts, obligations and claims shall be held illegal and void.

Section 5. The Congress shall have power to enforce, by appropriate legislation, the provisions of this article.

AMENDMENT XV
(1870)

Section 1. The right of citizens of the United States to vote shall not be denied or abridged by the United States or by any State on account of race, color, or previous condition of servitude.

Section 2. The Congress shall have power to enforce this article by appropriate legislation.

AMENDMENT XVI

The Congress shall have power to lay and collect taxes on incomes, from whatever source derived, without apportionment among the several States, and without regard to any census or enumeration.

AMENDMENT XVII
(1913)

Section 1. The Senate of the United States shall be composed of two Senators from each State, elected by the people thereof, for six years; and each Senator shall have one vote. The electors in each State shall have the qualifications requisite for electors of the most numerous branch of the State legislatures.

Section 2. When vacancies happen in the representation of any State in the Senate, the executive authority of such State shall issue writs of election to fill such vacancies: *Provided*, That the legislature of any State may empower the executive thereof to make temporary appointments until the people fill the vacancies by election as the legislature may direct.

Section 3. This amendment shall not be so construed as to affect the election or term of any Senator chosen before it becomes valid as part of the Constitution.

AMENDMENT XVIII
(1919)

Section 1. After one year from the ratification of this article the manufacture, sale, or transportation of intoxicating liquors within, the importation thereof into, or the exportation thereof from the United States and all territory subject to the jurisdiction thereof for beverage purposes is hereby prohibited.

Section 2. The Congress and the several States shall have concurrent power to enforce this article by appropriate legislation.

Section 3. This article shall be inoperative unless it shall have been ratified as an amendment to the Constitution by the legislatures of the several States as provided in the Constitution, within seven years of the date of the submission hereof to the States by Congress.

AMENDMENT XIX
(1920)

Section 1. The right of citizens of the United States to vote shall not be denied or abridged by the United States or by any State on account of sex.

appropriate legislation.

AMENDMENT XX
(1933)

Section 1. The terms of the President and Vice-President shall end at noon on the 20th day of January, and the terms of Senators and Representatives at noon on the 3d day of January, of the years in which such terms would have ended if this article had not been ratified; and the terms of their successors shall then begin.

Section 2. The Congress shall assemble at least once in every year, and such meeting shall begin at noon on the 3d day of January, unless they shall by law appoint a different day.

Section 3. If, at the time fixed for the beginning of the term of the President, the President elect shall have died, the Vice President elect shall become President. If a President shall not have been chosen before the time fixed for the beginning of his term, or if the President elect shall have failed to qualify, then the Vice President elect shall act as President until a President shall have qualified; and the Congress may by law provide for the case wherein neither a President elect nor a Vice President elect shall have qualified, declaring who shall then act as President, or the manner in which one who is to act shall be selected, and such person shall act accordingly until a President or Vice President shall have qualified.

Section 4. The Congress may by law provide for the case of the death of any of the persons from whom the House of Representatives may choose a President whenever the right of choice shall have devolved upon them, and for the case of the death of any of the persons from whom the Senate may choose a Vice President whenever the right of choice shall have devolved upon them.

Section 5. Sections 1 and 2 shall take effect on the 15th day of October following the ratification of this article.

Section 6. This article shall be inoperative unless it shall have been ratified as an amendment to the Constitution by three-fourths of the several States within seven years from the date of its submission.

AMENDMENT XXI
(1933)

Section 1. The eighteenth article of amendment to the Constitution of the United States is hereby repealed.

possession of the United States for delivery or use therein of intoxicating liquors, in violation of the laws thereof, is hereby prohibited.

Section 3. This article shall be inoperative unless it shall have been ratified as an amendment to the Constitution by conventions in the several States, as provided in the Constitution, within seven years from the date of the submission hereof to the States by the Congress.

AMENDMENT XXII
(1951)

Section 1. No person shall be elected to the office of the President more than twice, and no person who has held the office of President, or acted as President, for more than two years of a term to which some other person was elected President shall be elected to the office of the President more than once.

Section 2. But this Article shall not prevent any person holding the office of President when this Article was proposed by the Congress, and shall not apply to any person who may be holding the office of President, or acting as President, during the term within which this Article becomes operative from holding the office of President or acting as President during the remainder of such term.

This Article shall be inoperative unless it shall have been ratified as an amendment to the Constitution by the legislatures of three-fourths of the several States within seven years from the date of its submission to the States by the Congress.

AMENDMENT XXIII
(1961)

Section 1. The District constituting the seat of Government of the United States shall appoint in such manner as the Congress may direct:

A number of electors of President and Vice President equal to the whole number of Senators and Representative in Congress to which the District would be entitled if it were a State, but in no event more than the least populous State; they shall be in addition to those appointed by the States, but they shall be considered, for the purposes of the election of President and Vice President, to be electors appointed by a State; and they shall meet in the District and perform such duties as provided by the twelfth article of amendment.

AMENDMENT XXIV
(1964)

Section 1. The right of citizens of the United States to vote in any primary or other election for President or Vice President, for electors for President or Vice President, or for Senator or Representative in Congress, shall not be denied or abridged by the United States or any State by reason of failure to pay any poll tax or other tax.

Section 2. The Congress shall have the power to enforce this article by appropriate legislation.

AMENDMENT XXV
(1967)

Section 1. In case of the removal of the President from office or of his death or resignation, the Vice President shall become President.

Section 2. Whenever there is a vacancy in the office of the Vice President, the President shall nominate a Vice President who shall take office upon confirmation by a majority vote of both Houses of Congress.

Section 3. Whenever the President transmits to the President pro tempore of the Senate and the Speaker of the House of Representatives his written declaration that he is unable to discharge the powers and duties of his office, and until he transmits to them a written declaration to the contrary, such powers and duties shall be discharged by the Vice President as Acting President.

Section 4. Whenever the Vice President and a majority of either the principal officers of the executive departments or of such other body as Congress may by law provide, transmit to the President pro tempore of the Senate and the Speaker of the House of Representatives their written declaration that the President is unable to discharge the powers and duties of his office, the Vice President shall immediately assume the powers and duties of the office as Acting President.

Thereafter, when the President transmits to the President pro tempore of the Senate and the Speaker of the House of Representatives his written declaration that no inability exists, he shall resume the powers and duties of his office unless the Vice President and a majority of either the principal officers of the executive department or of such other body as Congress may by law provide, transmit within four days to the President pro tempore of the Senate and the Speaker of the House of Representatives their written

forty-eight hours for that purpose if not in session. If the Congress, within twenty-one days after receipt of the latter written declaration, or, if Congress is not in session, within twenty-one days after Congress is required to assemble, determines by two-thirds vote of both Houses that the President is unable to discharge the powers and duties of his office, the Vice President shall continue to discharge the same as Acting President; otherwise, the President shall resume the powers and duties of his office.

AMENDMENT XXVI
(1971)

Section 1. The right of citizens of the United States, who are eighteen years of age or older, to vote shall not be denied or abridged by the United States or by any State on account of age.

Section 2. The Congress shall have the power to enforce this article by appropriate legislation.

AMENDMENT XXVII
(1992)

Section 1. No law varying the compensation for the services of the Senators and Representatives shall take effect, until an election of Representatives shall have intervened.

It is now proper to . . . enumerate the principal circumstances from which it may be inferred that manufacturing establishments not only occasion a positive augmentation of the produce and revenue of the society, but that they contribute essentially to rendering them greater than they could possibly be, without such establishments. These circumstances are:

1. The division of labor.
2. An extension of the use of machinery.
3. Additional employment to classes of the community not ordinarily engaged in the business.
4. The promotion of emigration from foreign countries.
5. The furnishing greater scope for the diversity of talents and dispositions, which discriminate men from each other.
6. The affording a more ample and variable field for enterprise.
7. The creating, in some instances, a new, and securing, in all, a more certain and steady demand for the surplus produce of the soil. . . .

Not only the wealth; but the independence and security of a country, appear to be materially connected with the prosperity of manufactures. Every nation, with a view to those great objects, ought to endeavor to possess within itself all the essentials of national supply. These comprise the means of subsistence, habitation, clothing, and defence. . . .

It is not uncommon to meet with an opinion, that, thought the promoting of manufactures may be the interest of a part of the Union, it is contrary to that of another part. The Northern and Southern regions are sometimes represented as having adverse interests in this respect. Those are called manufacturing, these agricultural States: and a species of opposition is imagined to subsist between the manufacturing and agricultural interests. . . .

A full view having now been taken of the inducements to the promotion of manufactures in the United States, . . . it is proper . . . to consider the means by which it may be effected. . . .

1. *Protecting duties - or duties on those foreign articles which are the rivals of the domestic ones intended to be encouraged. . . .*
2. *Prohibitions of rival articles, or duties equivalent to prohibitions. . . .*
3. *Prohibitions of the exportation of the materials of manufactures. . . .*
4. *Pecuniary Bounties. . . .*
5. *Premiums. . . .*
6. *The exemption of the materials of manufactures from duty. . . .*
7. *Drawbacks of the duties which are imposed on the materials of manufactures. . . .*

made in other countries, particularly, those which relate to machinery. . . .

9. Judicious regulations for the inspection of manufactured commodities. . . .
10. The facilitating of pecuniary remittances form place to place. . . .
11. The facilitating of the transportation of commodities. . . .

In countries where there is great private wealth, much may be effected by the voluntary contributions of patriotic individuals; but in a community situated like that of the United States, the public purse must apply the deficiency of private resource. In what can it be so useful, as in prompting and improving the efforts of industry?

THE NATURALIZATION ACT
June 18, 1798

SEC. 1. *Be it enacted* . . . , That no alien shall be admitted to become a citizen of the United States, or of any state, unless . . . he shall have declared his intention to become a citizen of the United States, five years, at least, before his admission, and shall, at the time of his application to be admitted, declare and prove, to the satisfaction of the court having jurisdiction in the case, that he has resided within the United States fourteen years...and within the state or territory five years.

THE ALIEN ACT
June 25, 1798

SEC. 1. *Be it enacted* . . . , That it shall be lawful for the President of the United States at any time during the continuance of this act, to *order* all such *aliens* as he shall judge dangerous to the peace and safety of the United States, or shall have reasonable grounds to suspect are concerned in any treasonable or secret machinations against the government thereof, to depart out of the territory of the United States, within such time as shall be expressed in such order.

THE SEDITION ACT
July 14, 1798

SEC. 1. *Be it enacted* . . . , That if any persons shall unlawfully combine or conspire together, with intent to oppose any measure or measures of the government of the United States, which are or shall be directed by proper authority, or to impede the operation of any law of the United States, or to intimidate or prevent any person holding a place or office in or under the government of the United States, from undertaking, performing or executing his trust or duty; and if any person or persons, with intent as aforesaid, shall counsel, advise or attempt to procure any insurrection, riot, unlawful assembly, or combination, whether such conspiracy, threatening, counsel, advice, or attempt shall have the proposed effect or not, he or they shall be deemed guilty of a high misdemeanor, and on conviction, before any court of the United States having jurisdiction thereof, shall be punished by a fine not exceeding five thousand dollars, and by imprisonment during a term not less than six months nor exceeding five years; and further, at the discretion of the court may be holden to find sureties for his good behavior in such sum, and for such time, as the said court may direct.

knowingly and willingly assist or aid in writing, printing, uttering or publishing any false, scandalous and malicious writing or writings against the government of the United States, or either house of the Congress of the United States, or the President of the United States, with intent to defame the said government, or either house of the said Congress, or the said President, or to bring them, or either of them, into contempt or disrepute; or to excite against them, or either or any of them, the hatred of the good people of the United States, or to stir up sedition within the United States, or to excite any unlawful combinations therein...Then such person being thereof convicted before any court of the United States having jurisdiction thereof shall be punished by a fine not exceeding two thousand dollars, and by imprisonment not exceeding two years.

That this act shall continue to be in force until March 3, 1801, and no longer. . . .

The first object of enquiry is,

1st. Has the applicant a right to the commission he demands? That by signing the commission of Mr. Marbury, the president of the United States appointed him a justice of peace for the county of Washington in the district of Columbia; and that the seal of the United States, affixed thereto by the secretary of state, is conclusive testimony of the verity of the signature, and of the completion of the appointment; and that the appointment conferred on him a legal right to the office for the space of five years.

2dly. If he has a right, and that right has been violated, do the laws of his country afford him a remedy?

The act (Judiciary Act 1789) to establish the judicial courts of the United States authorizes the supreme court "to issue writs of mandamus, in cases warranted by the principles and usages of law, to any courts appointed, or persons holding office, under the authority of the United. States."

The secretary of state, being a person holding an office under the authority of the United States is precisely within the letter of the description; and if this court is not authorized to issue a writ of mandamus to such an officer, it must be because the law is unconstitutional, and therefore absolutely incapable of conferring the authority and assigning the duties which its words purport to confer and assign.

The constitution vests the whole judicial power of the United States in one supreme court.

The authority, therefore, given to the supreme court, by the act establishing the judicial courts of the United States, to issue writs of mandamus to public officers, appears not to be warranted by the constitution.

The question whether an act repugnant to the constitution can become the law of the land, is a question deeply interesting to the United States . . .

It is emphatically the province and duty of the judicial department to say what the law is. Those who apply the rule to particular cases must of necessity expound and interpret that rule. If two laws conflict with each other, the courts must decide on the operation of each.

So if a law be in opposition to the constitution; if both the law and the constitution apply to a particular case, so that the court must either decide that case conformably to the law, disregarding the constitution, or

152

The judicial power of the United States is extended to all cases arising under the constitution.

It is also not entirely unworthy of observation, that in declaring what shall be the *supreme* law of the land, the constitution itself is first mentioned, and not the laws of the United States generally, but those only which shall be made in *pursuance* of the constitution, have that rank.

Thus, the particular phraseology of the constitution of the United States confirms and strengthens the principle, supposed to be essential to all written constitutions, that a law repugnant to the constitution is void, and that courts, as well as other department, are bound by that instrument.

3dly. If they do afford him a remedy, is it *a mandamus* issuing from this court? . . .

Mandamus denied.

Approved 7-0

PREAMBLE

The people of Connecticut acknowledging with gratitude, the good providence of God, in having permitted them to enjoy a free government; do, in order more effectually to define, secure, and perpetuate the liberties, rights and privileges which they have derived from their ancestors; hereby, after a careful consideration and revision, ordain and establish the following constitution and form of civil government.

ARTICLE FIRST
Declaration of Rights

That the great and essential principles of liberty and free government may be recognized and established,

WE DECLARE,

Sec. 1. That all men when they form a social compact, are equal in rights; and that no man, or set of men are entitled to exclusive public emoluments or privileges from the community.

Sec. 2. That all political power is inherent in the people, and all free governments are founded on their authority, and instituted for their benefit; and that they have at all times an undeniable and indefeasible right to alter their form of government in such manner as they may think expedient.

Sec. 3. The exercise and enjoyment of religious profession and worship, without discrimination, shall forever be free to all persons in this state; provided, that the right hereby declared and established, shall not be so construed as to excuse acts of licentiousness, or to justify practices inconsistent with the peace and safety of the state.

Sec. 4. No preference shall be given by law to any Christian sect or mode of worship.

Sec. 5. Every citizen may freely speak, write and publish his sentiments on all subjects, being responsible for the abuse of that liberty.

Sec. 6. No law shall ever be passed to curtail or restrain the liberty of speech or of the press.

Sec. 7. In all prosecutions or indictments for libels, the truth may be given in evidence, and the jury shall have the right to determine the law and the facts, under the direction of the court.

Sec. 8. The people shall be secure in their persons, houses, papers and possessions from unreasonable searches or seizures; and no warrant to search any place, or to seize any person or things, shall issue without describing them as nearly as may be, nor without probable cause supported by oath or affirmation.

Sec. 9. In all criminal prosecutions, the accused shall have a right to be heard by himself and by counsel; to demand the nature and cause of the accusation; to be confronted by the witnesses against him; to have compulsory process to obtain witnesses in his favor; and in all prosecutions by indictment or information, a speedy, public trial by an impartial jury. He shall not be compelled to give evidence against himself, nor be deprived of life, liberty or property, but by due course of law. And no person shall be holden to answer for any crime, the punishment of which may be death or imprisonment for life, unless on a presentment or an indictment of a grand jury; except in the land or naval forces, or in the militia when in actual service in time of war, or public danger.

Sec. 10. No person shall be arrested, detained or punished, except in cases clearly warranted by law.

Sec. 11. The property of no person shall be taken for public use, without just compensation therefor.

Sec. 12. All courts shall be open, and every person, for an injury done to him in his person, property or reputation, shall have remedy by due course of law, and right and justice administered without sale, denial or delay.

Sec. 13. Excessive bail shall not be required, nor excessive fines imposed.

Sec. 14. All prisoners shall, before conviction, be bailable by sufficient sureties, except for capital offenses, where the proof is evident, or the presumption great; and the privileges of the writ of habeas corpus shall not be suspended, unless, when in case of rebellion or invasion, the public safety may require it; nor in any case, but by the legislature.

Sec. 15. No person shall be attainted of treason or felony, by the legislature.

Sec. 16. The citizens have a right, in a peaceable manner, to assemble for their common good, and to apply to those invested with the powers of government, for redress of grievances, or other proper purposes, by petition, address or remonstrance.

Sec. 17. Every citizen has a right to bear arms in defense of himself and the state.

Sec. 18. The military shall, in all cases, and at all times, be in strict subordination to the civil power.

Sec. 19. No soldier shall, in time of peace, be quartered in any house, without the consent of the owner; nor in time of war, but in a manner to be prescribed by law.

Sec. 20. No hereditary emoluments, privileges or honors, shall ever be granted, or conferred in this state.

Sec. 21. The right of trial by jury shall remain inviolate.

MISSOURI CRISIS AND IMPACT
April 22, 1820

I thank you, dear Sir, for the copy you have been so kind as to send me of the letter to your constituents on the Missouri question. It is a perfect justification to them. I had for a long time ceased to read newspapers, or pay any attention to public affairs, confident they were in good hands, and content to be a passenger in our bark to the shore from which I am not distant. But this momentous question, like a fire-ball in the night, awakened and filled me with terror. I considered it at once as the knell of the Union. It is hushed, indeed, for the moment. But this is a reprieve only, not a final sentence. A geographical line, coinciding with a marked principle, moral and political, once conceived and held up to the angry passions of men, will never be obliterated; and every new irritation will mark it deeper. I can say, with conscious truth, that there is not a man on earth who would sacrifice more than I would to relieve us from this heavy reproach, in any practicable way. The cession of that kind of property, for so it is misnamed, is a bagatelle which would not cost me a second thought, if, in that way, a general emancipation and expatriation could be affected; and, gradually, and with due sacrifices, I think it might be. But as it is, we have the wolf by the ears, and we can neither hold him, nor safely let him go. Justice is in one scale, and self-preservation in the other.

Of one thing I am certain, that as the passage of slaves from one State to another, would not make a slave of a single human being who would not be so without it, so their diffusion over a greater surface would make them individually happier, and proportionally facilitate the accomplishment of their emancipation, by dividing the burden on a greater number of coadjutors. An abstinence too, from this act of power, would remove the jealousy excited by the undertaking of Congress to regulate the condition of the different descriptions of men composing a State. This certainly is the exclusive right of every State, which nothing in the Constitution has taken from them and given to the General Government. Could Congress, for example, say, that the non-freemen of Connecticut shall be freemen, or that they shall not emigrate into any other State?

I regret that I am now to die in the belief, that the useless sacrifice of themselves by the generation of 1776, to acquire self-government and happiness to their country, is to be thrown away by the unwise and unworthy passions of their sons, and that my only consolation is to be that I live not to weep over it. If they would but dispassionately weigh the blessings they will throw away, against an abstract principle more likely to be effected by union than by scission, they would pause before they would perpetrate this act of suicide on themselves, and of treason against the hopes of the world. To yourself, as the faithful advocate of the Union, I tender the offering of my high esteem and respect.

In the previous document, Thomas Jefferson expressed his growing concern over slavery and the impending difficulties he envisioned for the nation because of the adoption of the Compromise of 1820.

In this document, usually referred to as the "firebell in the night" letter, Jefferson defined his solution to the problem of slavery in America. While he never defended slavery, he, like many contemporaries, could not conceive of a society in which African-Americans could be free and equal to whites.

What makes this letter so significant is that Jefferson confides his fears for the nation at the same time that he indicates his life-long solution to the dilemma of slavery. What precisely does he mean by "emancipation and expatriation?"

JAMES MONROE, MESSAGE TO CONGRESS
December, 1823

At the proposal of the Russian Imperial Government . . . a full power and instructions have been transmitted to the minister of the United States at St. Petersburg to arrange by amicable negotiation the respective rights and interests of the two nations on the northwest coast of this continent. A similar proposal has been made . . . to the Government of Great Britain, which has likewise been acceded to. The Government of the United States has been desirous by this friendly proceeding of manifesting . . . their solicitude to cultivate the best understanding with his [the Russian] Government. In the discussions to which this interest has given rise and in the arrangements by which they may terminate, the occasion has been judged proper for asserting, as a principle in which the rights and interests of the United States are involved, that the American continents, by the free and independent condition which they have assumed and maintain, are henceforth not to be considered as subjects for future colonization by any European powers. . . .

In the wars of the European powers, in matters relating to themselves, we have never taken any part, nor does it comport with our policy so to do. It is only when our rights are invaded or seriously menaced that we resent injuries or make preparations for our defense. With the movements in this hemisphere we are of necessity more immediately connected, and by causes which must be obvious to all enlightened and impartial observers. The political system of the allied powers is essentially different in this respect from that of America. This difference proceeds from that which exists in their respective Governments; and to the defense of our own, which has been achieved by the loss of so much blood and treasure, and matured by the wisdom of their most enlightened citizens, and under which we have enjoyed unexampled felicity, this whole nation is devoted. We owe it, therefore, to candor, and to the amicable relations existing between the United States and those powers, to declare that we should consider any attempt on their part to extend their system, to any portion of this hemisphere, as dangerous to our peace and safety. With the existing colonies or dependencies of any European power we have not interfered and shall not interfere. But with the Governments who have declared their independence and maintained it, and whose independence we have, on great consideration and on just principles, acknowledged, we could not view any interposition for the purpose of oppressing them, or controlling in any other manner their destiny, by any European power, in any other light than as the manifestation of an unfriendly disposition toward the United States.

ANDREW JACKSON ENDORSES THE INDIAN REMOVAL
1829

The condition and ulterior destiny of the Indian tribes within the limits of some of our states have become objects of much interest and importance. It has long been the policy of government to introduce among them the arts of civilization, in the hope of gradually reclaiming them from a wandering life. This policy has, however, been coupled with another wholly incompatible with its success. Professing a desire to civilize and settle them, we have at the same time lost no opportunity to purchase their lands and thrust them farther into the wilderness. By this means they have not only been kept in a wandering state, but been led to look upon us as unjust and indifferent to their fate. . . .

Our conduct toward these people is deeply interesting to our national character. Their present condition, contrasted with what they once were, makes a most powerful appeal to our sympathies. Our ancestors found them the uncontrolled possessors of these vast regions. By persuasion and force they have been made to retire from river to river and from mountain to mountain, until some of the tribes have become extinct and others have left but remnants to preserve for awhile their once terrible names. Surrounded by the whites with their arts of civilization, which, by destroying the resources of the savage, doom him to weakness and decay, the fate of the Mohegan, the Narrangansett, and the Delaware is fast overtaking the Choctaw, the Cherokee, and the Creek. That this fate surely awaits them if they remain within the limits of the states does not admit of a doubt. Humanity and national honor demand that every effort should be made to avert so great a calamity. . . .

As a means of effecting this end, I suggest for your consideration the propriety of setting apart an ample district west of the Mississippi, and without [outside] the limits of any state or territory now formed, to be guaranteed to the Indian tribes as long as they shall occupy it, each tribe having a distinct control over the portion designated for its use. There they may be secured in the enjoyment of governments of their own choice, subject to no other control from the United States than such as may be necessary to preserve peace on the frontier and between the several tribes. There the benevolent may endeavor to teach them the arts of civilization, and by promoting union and harmony among them, to raise up an interesting commonwealth, destined to perpetuate the race and to attest the humanity and justice of this government.

This emigration should be voluntary, for it would be as cruel as unjust to compel the aborigines to abandon the graves of their fathers and seek a home in a distant land. But they should be distinctly informed that if they remain within the limits of the states they must be subject to their laws.

ANDREW JACKSON, VETOES THE BANK
1832

. . . It is to be regretted that the rich and powerful too often bend the acts of government to their selfish purposes. Distinctions in society will always exist under every just government. Equality of talents, of education, or of wealth can not be produced by human institutions. In the full enjoyment of the gifts of Heaven and the fruits of superior industry, economy, and virtue, every man is equally entitled to protection by law; but when the laws undertake to add to these natural and just advantages artificial distinctions, to grant titles, gratuities, and exclusive privileges, to make the rich richer and the potent more powerful, the humble members of society - the farmers, mechanics, and labors - who have neither the time nor the means of securing like favors to themselves, have a right to complain of the injustice of their Government.

. . . Many of our rich men have not been content with equal protection and equal benefits, but have besought us to make them richer by act of Congress. By attempting to gratify their desires we have in the results of our legislation arrayed section against section, interest against interest, and man against man, in a fearful commotion which threatened to shake the foundations of our Union." There are no necessary evils in government. Its evils exist only in its abuses. If it would confine itself to equal protection, and, as Heaven does its rains, shower its favors alike on the high and the low, the rich and the poor, it would be an unqualified blessing. In the act before me there seems to be a wide and unnecessary departure from these just principles. . . .

THE SENECA FALLS DECLARATION OF SENTIMENTS
AND RESOLUTIONS
July 19, 1848

1. Declaration of Sentiments

When, in the course of human events, it becomes necessary for one portion of the family of man to assume among the people of the earth a position different from that which they have hitherto occupied, but one to which the laws of nature and of nature's God entitle them, a decent respect to the opinions of mankind requires that they should declare the causes that impel them to such a course.

We hold these truths to be self-evident: that all men and women are created equal; that they are endowed by their Creator with certain inalienable rights; that among these are life, liberty, and the pursuit of happiness; that to secure these rights governments are instituted, deriving their just powers from the consent of the governed. Whenever any form of government becomes destructive of these ends, it is the right of those who suffer from it to refuse allegiance to it, and to insist upon the institution of a new government, laying its foundation on such principles, and organizing its powers in such form, as to them shall seem most likely to effect their safety and happiness. Prudence, indeed, will dictate that governments long established should not be changed for light and transient causes; and accordingly all experience hath shown that mankind are more disposed to suffer while evils are sufferable, than to right themselves by abolishing the forms to which they are accustomed. But when a long train of abuses and usurpations, pursuing invariably the same object, envinces a design to reduce them under absolute despotism, it is their duty to throw off such government, and such is now the necessity which constrains them to demand the equal station to which they are entitled.

The history of mankind is a history of repeated injuries and usurpations on the part of man toward woman, having in direct object the establishment of an absolute tyranny over her. To prove this, let facts be submitted to a candid world.

He has never permitted her to exercise her inalienable right to the elective franchise.

He has compelled her to submit to laws, in the formation of which she had no voice.

He has withheld from her rights which are given to the most ignorant and degraded men -- both natives and foreigners.

Having deprived her of this first right of a citizen, the elective franchise, thereby leaving her without representation in the halls of legislation, he has oppressed her on all sides.

He has made her, if married, in the eye of the law, civilly dead.

He has taken from her all right in property, even to the wages she earns.

He has made her, morally, an irresponsible being, as she can commit many crimes with impunity, provided they be done in the presence of her husband. In the covenant of marriage, she is compelled to promise obedience to her husband, he becoming, to all intents and purposes, her master -- the law giving him power to deprive her of her liberty, and to administer chastisement.

He has so framed the laws of divorce, as to what shall be the proper causes, and in case of separation, to whom the guardianship of the children shall be given, as to wholly regardless of the happiness of women -- the law, in all cases, going upon a false supposition of the supremacy of man, and giving all power into his hands.

After depriving her of all rights as a married woman, if single, and the owner of property, he has taxed her to support a government which recognizes her only when her property can be made profitable to it.

He has monopolized nearly all the profitable employments, and from those she is permitted to follow, she receives but a scanty remuneration. He closes against her all the avenues to wealth and distinction which he considers most honorable to himself. As a teacher of theology, medicine, or law, she is not known.

He has denied her the facilities for obtaining a thorough education, all colleges being closed against her.

He allows her in Church, as well as State, but a subordinate position, claiming Apostolic authority for her exclusion from the ministry, and, with some exceptions, from any public participation in the affairs of the Church.

He has created a false public sentiment by giving to the world a different code of morals for men and women, by which moral delinquencies which exclude women from society, are not only tolerated, but deemed of little account in man.

He has usurped the prerogative of Jehovah himself, claiming it as his right to assign for her a sphere of action, when that belongs to her conscience and to her God.

He has endeavored, in every way that he could, to destroy her confidence in her own powers, to lessen her self-respect and to make her willing to lead a dependent and abject life.

Now, in view of this entire disfranchisement of one-half the people of this country, their social and religious degradation -- in view of the unjust laws above mentioned, and because women do feel themselves aggrieved, oppressed, and fraudulently deprived of their most sacred rights, we insist that they have immediate admission to all the rights and privileges which belong to them as citizens of the United States.

In entering upon the great work before us, we anticipate no small amount of misconception, misrepresentation, and ridicule but we shall use every instrumentality within our power to effect our object. We shall employ agents, circulate tracts, petition the State and National legislatures, and endeavor to enlist the pulpit and the press in our behalf. We hope this Convention will be followed by a series of Conventions embracing every part of the country.

2. Resolutions

Whereas, The great precept of nature is conceded to be, that "man shall pursue his own true and substantial happiness." Blackstone in his Commentaries remarks, that this law of Nature being coeval with mankind, and dictated by God himself, is of course superior in obligation to any other. It is binding over all the globe, in all countries and at all times; no human laws are of any validity if contrary to this, and such of them as are valid, derive all their force, and all their validity, and all their authority, mediately and immediately, from this original; therefore,

Resolved, That all laws which prevent woman from occupying such a station in society as her conscience shall dictate, or which place her in a position inferior to that of man, are contrary to the great precept of nature, and therefore of no force or authority.

Resolved, That woman is man's equal -- was intended to be so by the Creator, and the highest good of the race demands that she should be recognized as such.

Resolved, That inasmuch as man, while claiming for himself intellectual superiority, does accord to woman moral superiority, it is pre-eminently his duty to encourage her to speak and teach, as she has an opportunity, in all religious assemblies.

Resolved, That the same amount of virtue, delicacy, and refinement of behavior that is required of woman in the social state, should also be required of man, and the same transgressions should be visited with equal severity on both man and woman.

Resolved, That the objection of indelicacy and impropriety, which is so often brought against woman when she addresses a public audience, comes with a very ill-grace from those who encourage, by their attendance, her appearance on the stage, in the concert, or in feats of the circus.

Resolved, That woman has too long rested satisfied in the circumscribed limits which corrupt customs and a perverted application of the Scriptures have marked out for her, and that it is time she should move in the enlarged sphere which her great Creator has assigned her.

Resolved, That it is the duty of the women of this country to secure to themselves their sacred right to the elective franchise.

Resolved, That the equality of human rights results necessarily from the fact of the identity of the race in capabilities and responsibilities.

Resolved, That the speedy success of our cause depends upon the zealous and untiring efforts of both men and women, for the overthrow of the monopoly of the pulpit, and for the securing to women an equal participation with men in the various trades, professions, and commerce.

DRED SCOTT v. SANDFORD
March, 1857

This is certainly a very serious question, and one that now for the first time has been brought for decision before this court. But it is brought here by those who have a right to bring it, and it is our duty to meet it and decide it.

The question is simply this: Can a negro, whose ancestors were imported into this country, and sold as slaves, become a member of the political community formed and brought into existence by the Constitution of the United States, and as such become entitled to all the rights, and privileges, and immunities, guarantied by that instrument to the citizen? One of which rights is the privilege of suing in a court of the United States in the cases specified in the Constitution.

It will be observed that the plea applies to that class of persons only whose ancestors were negroes of the African race, and imported into this country, and sold and held as slaves. The only matter in issue before the court, therefore, is, whether the descendants of such slaves, when they shall be emancipated, or who are born of parents who had become free before their birth, are citizens of a State, in the sense in which the word citizen is used in the Constitution of the United States. And this being the only matter in dispute on the pleadings, the court must be understood as speaking in this opinion of that class only, that is of persons who are the descendants of Africans who were imported into this country and sold as slaves. . . .

The question before us is, whether the class of persons described in the plea in abatement compose a portion of this people, and are constituent members of this sovereignty? We think they are not, and that they are not included, and were not intended to be included, under the word "citizens" in the Constitution, and can, therefore, claim none of the rights and privileges which that instrument provides for and secures to citizens of the United States. On the contrary, they were at that time considered as a subordinate and inferior class of beings, who had been subjugated by the dominant race, and whether emancipated or not, yet remained subject to their authority, and had no rights or privileges but such as those who held the power and the government might choose to grant them. . . .

It becomes necessary, therefore, to determine who were citizens of the several States when the Constitution was adopted.

In the opinion of the court, the legislation and histories of the times, and the language used in the Declaration of Independence, show, that neither the class of persons who had been imported as slaves, nor their descendants, whether they had become free or not, were then acknowledged as a part of the people, nor intended to be included in the general words used in that memorable instrument.

They had for more than a century before been regarded as beings of an inferior order; and altogether unfit to associate with the white race, either in social or political relations; and so far inferior that they had no rights which the white man was bound to respect; and that the negro might justly and lawfully be reduced to slavery for his benefit. . . . This opinion was at that time fixed and universal in the civilized portion of the white race. It was regarded as an axiom in morals as well as in politics, which no one thought of disputing, or supposed to be open to dispute; and men in every grade and position in society daily and habitually acted upon it in their private pursuits, as well as in matters of public concern, without doubting for a moment the correctness of this opinion. . . .

And upon a full and careful consideration of the subject, the court is of opinion that, upon the facts stated in the plea in abatement, Dred Scott was not a citizen of Missouri within the meaning of the Constitution of the United States, and not entitled as such to sue in its courts and consequently, that the Circuit Court had no jurisdiction of the case, and that the judgment on the plea in abatement is erroneous. . . .

We proceed, therefore, to inquire whether the facts relied on by the plaintiff entitled him to his freedom. . . .

In considering this part of the controversy, two questions arise: 1st. Was he, together with his family, free in Missouri by reason of the stay in the territory of the United States hereinbefore mentioned? And 2d, If they were not, is Scott himself free by reason of his removal to Rock Island, in the State of Illinois, as stated in the above admissions?

Thus the rights of property are united with the rights of person, and placed on the same ground by the fifth amendment to the Constitution. . . . An Act of Congress which deprives a person of the United States of his liberty or property merely because he came himself or brought his property into a particular Territory of the United States, and who had committed no offense against the laws, could hardly be dignified with the name of due process of law. . . .

But . . . if the Constitution recognizes the right of property of the master in a slave, and makes no distinction between that description of property and other property owned by a citizen, no tribunal, acting under the authority of the United States, whether it be legislative, executive, or judicial, has a right to draw such a distinction, or deny to it the benefit of the provisions and guarantees which have been provided for the protection of private property against the encroachments of the Government.

Now . . . the right of property in a slave is distinctly and expressly affirmed the Constitution. The right to traffic in it, like an ordinary article of merchandise and property, was guaranteed to the citizens of the United States, in every State that might desire it, for twenty years. And the Government in express terms is pledged to protect it in all future time, if the slave escapes form his owner.

The only power conferred is the power coupled with the duty of guarding and protecting the owner in his rights.

Upon these considerations, it is the opinion of the court that the Act of Congress which prohibited a citizen from holding and owning property of this kind in the territory of the United States north of the line therein mentioned, is not warranted by the Constitution, and is therefore void; and that neither Dred Scott himself, nor any of his family, were made free by being carried into this territory.

5-2 Approved

SLAVERY IN THE SOUTH
1820-1860

	Female	Male	TOTAL
1820	750,010	788,028	1,538,028
1830	996,220	1,012,823	1,999,043
1840	1,240,938	1,246,517	2,487,455
1850	1,601,779	1,602,534	3,204,313
1860	1,971,135	1,982,625	3,953,760

Although the importation of slaves from Africa and the Caribbean was banned as of January 1, 1808, it has been estimated that some 54,000 slaves were illegally brought into the US between 1808 and 1861 when the South seceded from the union and began the Civil War.

DISTRIBUTION OF SLAVES BY 1860

Percent of White Families	Number of Slaves Held	Percent Of Slaves Held
75	0	0
1	40 or more	31
9	7-39	53
15	1-6	16

In 1860, 25 percent of the total white population or some 283,000 families, held close to 4 million human slaves.

US Bureau of Census, Historical Statistics of the US: Colonial Times to 1970. (US Government Printing Office, 1957), p. 18. Series 119-134 [population by age, sex, race and nativity, 1790-1970]

LINCOLN-DOUGLAS DEBATE
Mr. Stephen Douglas -August 21, 1858

Mr. Lincoln . . . says that this Government cannot endure permanently in the same condition in which it was made by its framers -- divided into free and slave States. He says that it has existed for about seventy years thus divided, and yet he tells you that it cannot endure permanently on the same principles and in the same relative condition in which our fathers made it. Why can it not exist divided into free and slave States? Washington, Jefferson, Franklin, Madison, Hamilton, Jay, and the great men of that day made this Government divided into free States and slave States, and left each State perfectly free to do as it pleased on the subject of slavery. Why can it not exist on the same principles on which our fathers made it? They knew when they framed the Constitution that in a country as wide and broad as this, with such a variety of climate, production and interest, the people necessarily required different laws and institutions in different localities. They knew that the laws and regulations which would suit the granite hills of New Hampshire would be unsuited to the rice plantations of South Carolina, and they, therefore, provided that each State should retain its own legislature and its own sovereignty with the full and complete power to do as it pleased within its own limits, in all that was local and not national. One of the reserved rights of the States, was the right to regulate the relation between master and servant, on the slavery question. At the time the Constitution was framed, there were thirteen States in the Union, twelve of which were slaveholding States and one a free State. Suppose this doctrine of uniformity preached by Mr. Lincoln, that the States should all be free or all be slave, had prevailed, and what would have been the result? Of course, the twelve slaveholding States would have overruled the one free State, and slavery would have been fastened by a Constitutional provision on every inch of the American Republic, instead of being left as our fathers wisely left it, to each State to decide for itself. Here I assert that uniformity in the local laws and institutions of the different States is neither possible or desirable. If uniformity had been adopted when the Government was established, it must inevitably have been the uniformity of slavery everywhere, or else the uniformity of Negro citizenship and Negro equality everywhere.

We are told by Lincoln that he is utterly opposed to the Dred Scott decision, and will not submit to it, for the reason that he says it deprives the Negro of the rights and privileges of citizenship. That is the first and main reason which he assigns for his warfare on the Supreme Court of the United States and its decision. I ask you, are you in favor of conferring upon the Negro the rights and privileges of citizenship? Do you desire to strike out of our State Constitution that clause which keeps slaves and free Negroes out of the State, and allow the free Negroes to flow in, and cover your prairies with black settlements? Do you desire to turn this beautiful State into a free Negro colony, in order that when Missouri abolishes slavery she can send one hundred thousand emancipated slave into Illinois, to become citizens and voters, on an equality with yourselves? If you desire Negro citizenship, if you desire to allow them to come into the State and settle with the white man, if you desire them to vote on an equality with yourselves, and to make them eligible to office, to serve on juries, and to adjudge your rights, then support Mr. Lincoln and the Black Republican party, who are in favor of the citizenship of the Negro. For one, I am opposed to Negro citizenship in any and every form. I believe this Government was made on the white basis. I believe it was made by white men, for the benefit of white men and their posterity forever, and I am in favor of confining citizenship to white men, men of European birth and descent, instead of conferring it upon Negroes, Indians, and other inferior races.

Mr. Abraham Lincoln - October 15, 1858

. . The real issue in this controversy -- the one pressing upon every mind --- is the sentiment on the part of one class that looks upon the institution of slavery *as a wrong*, and of another class that *does not* look upon it as a wrong. The sentiment that contemplates the institution of slavery in this country as a wrong is the sentiment of the Republican party. It is the sentiment around which all their actions, all their arguments, circle, from which all their propositions radiate. They look upon it as being a moral, social, and political wrong; and while they contemplate it as such, they nevertheless have due regard for its actual existence among us the difficulties of getting rid of it in any satisfactory way, and to all the constitutional obligations thrown about it. Yet, having a due regard for these, they desire a policy in regard to it that looks to its not creating any more danger. They insist that it should, as far as may be, *be treated* as a wrong; and one of the methods of treating it as a wrong is to *make provision that it shall grow no larger*.

I repeat it here, that if there be a man amongst us who does not think that the institution of slavery is wrong in any one of the aspects of which I have spoken, he is misplaced, and ought not to be with us. And if there be a man amongst us who is so impatient of it as a wrong as to disregard its actual presence among us and the difficulty of getting rid of it suddenly in a satisfactory way, and to disregard the constitutional obligations thrown about it, that man is misplaced if he is on our platform. We disclaim sympathy with him in practical action. He is not placed properly with us.

Has anything ever threatened the existence of this Union save and except this very institution of slavery? What is it that we hold most dear amongst us? Our own liberty and prosperity. What has ever threatened our liberty and prosperity, save and except this institution of slavery? If this is true, how do you propose to improve the condition of things by enlarging slavery, -- by spreading it out and making it bigger? You may have a wen or cancer upon your person, and not be able to cut it out, lest you bleed to death; but surely it is no way to cure it, to engraft it and spread it over your whole body. That is no proper way of treating what you regard a wrong.

On the other hand, I have said there is a sentiment which treats it as *not* being wrong. That is the Democratic sentiment of this day. . . .

. . . The Democratic policy in regard to that institution will not tolerate the merest breath, the slightest hint, of the least degree of wrong about it. Try it by some of Judge Douglas's arguments. He says, he, "don't care whether it is voted up or voted down" in the Territories. I do not care myself, in dealing with that expression, whether it is intended to be expressive of his individual sentiments on the subject, or only of the national policy he desires to have established. It is alike valuable for my purpose. Any man can say that who does not see anything wrong in slavery; but no man can logically say it who does see a wrong in it, because no man can logically say he don't care whether a wrong is voted up or voted down, but he must logically have a choice between a right thing and a wrong thing. He contends that whatever community wants slaves has a right to have them. So they have, if it is not a wrong. But if it is a wrong, he cannot say people have a right to do wrong. He says that upon the score of equality slaves should be allowed to go in a new Territory, like other property. This is strictly logical if there is no difference between it and other property. If it and other property are equal, this argument is entirely logical. But if you insist that one is wrong and the other right, there is no use to institute a comparison between right and wrong. You may turn over everything in the Democratic policy from beginning to end, whether in the shape it takes on the statute book, in the shape it takes in the Dred Scott decision, in the shape it takes in conversation, or the shape it takes in short maxim-like arguments, -- it everywhere carefully excludes the idea that there is anything wrong in it.

That is the real issue. That is the issue that will continue in this country when these poor tongues of Judge Douglas and myself shall be silent. It is the eternal struggle between these two principles -- right and wrong -- throughout the world. They are the two principles that have stood face to face from the beginning of time, and will ever continue to struggle. The one is the common right of humanity, and the other the divine right of kings. . . . And whenever we can get rid of the fog which obscures the real question, when we can get Judge Douglas and his friends to avow a policy looking to its perpetuation, -- we can get out from among that class of men and bring them to the side of those who treat it as a wrong. Then there will soon be an end of it, and that end will be its "ultimate extinction."

STATE OF MISSISSIPPI - ORDERS OF SECESSION
January 26, 1861

Our position is thoroughly identified with the institution of slavery -- the greatest material interest of the world. Its labor supplies the product which constitutes by far the largest and most important portions of the commerce of the earth. These products are peculiar to the climate verging on the tropical regions, and by an imperious law of nature none but the black race can bear exposure to the tropical sun. These products have become necessities of the world, and a blow at slavery is a blow at commerce and civilization. That blow has been long aimed at the institution and was at the point of reaching its consummation. There was no choice left us but submission to the mandates of abolition or a dissolution of the Union, whose principles had been subverted to work out our ruin.

That we do not overstate the dangers to our institutions, a reference to a few unquestionable facts will sufficiently prove.

The hostility to this institution commenced before the adoption of the Constitution, and was manifested in the well-known Ordinance of 1787 in regard to the Northwestern Territory.

The feeling increased until in 1819-20 it deprived the South of more than half the vast territory acquired from France.

The same hostility dismembered Texas and seized upon all the territory acquired from Mexico.

It has grown until it denies the right of property in slaves, and refuses protection to that right on the high seas, in the Territories, and wherever the government of the United States has jurisdiction.

It refuses the admission of new slave States into the Union, and seeks to extinguish it by confining it within its present limits, denying the power of expansion.

It tramples the original equality of the South underfoot.

It has nullified the Fugitive Slave Law in almost every free State in the Union, and has utterly broken the compact which our fathers pledged their faith to maintain.

It advocates Negro equality, socially and politically, and promotes insurrection and incendiarism in our midst.

It has enlisted the press, its pulpit, and its schools against us until the whole popular mind of the North is excited and inflamed with prejudice.

It has made combinations and formed associations to carry out its schemes of emancipation in the States and wherever else slavery exists.

It seeks not to elevate or to support the slave, but to destroy his present condition without providing a better.

It has invaded a State, and invested with the honors of martyrdom the wretch whose purpose was to apply flames to our dwellings and the weapons of destruction to our lives.

It has broken every compact into which it has entered for our security.

It has given indubitable evidence of its design to ruin our agriculture, to prostrate our industrial pursuits, and to destroy our social system.

It knows no relenting or hesitation in its purposes: it stops not in its march of aggression, and leaves us no room to hope for cessation or for pause.

It has recently obtained control of the Government by the prosecution of its unhallowed schemes, and destroyed the last expectation of living together in friendship and brotherhood.

Utter subjugation awaits us in the Union, if we should consent longer to remain in it. It is not a matter of choice, but of necessity. We must either submit to degradation and to loss of property worth four billions of money, or we must secede from the Union framed by our fathers, to secure this as well as every other species of property. For far less cause than this our fathers separated from the Crown of England.

Our decision is made. We follow in their footsteps. We embrace the alternative of separation, and for the reasons here stated, we resolve to maintain our rights with the full consciousness of the justice of our course and the undoubting belief of our ability to maintain it.

THE GETTYSBURG ADDRESS
November 19, 1863

Four score and seven years ago our fathers brought forth on this continent, a new nation, conceived in Liberty, and dedicated to the proposition that all men are created equal.

Now we are engaged in a great civil war, testing whether that nation or any nation so conceived and so dedicated, can long endure. We are met on a great battle-field of that war. We have come to dedicate a portion of that field, as a final resting place for those who here gave their lives that that nation might live. It is altogether fitting and proper that we should do this.

But, in a larger sense, we can not dedicate -- we can not consecrate -- we can not hallow -- this ground. The brave men, living and dead, who struggled here, have consecrated it, far above our poor power to add or detract. The world will little note, nor long remember what we say here, but it can never forget what they did here. It is for us the living, rather, to be dedicated here to the unfinished work which they who fought here have thus far so nobly advanced. It is rather for us to be here dedicated to the great task remaining before us -- that from these honored dead we take increased devotion to that cause for which they gave the last full measure of devotion -- that we here highly resolve that these dead shall not have died in vain -- that this nation, under God, shall have a new birth of freedom -- and that government of the people, by the people, for the people, shall not perish from the earth.

ABRAHAM LINCOLN, SECOND INAUGURAL ADDRESS
March 4, 1865

FELLOW-COUNTRYMEN: -- At this second appearing to take the oath of the presidential office there is less occasion for an extended address than there was at the first.

One eighth of the whole population was colored slaves, not distributed generally over the Union, but localized in the southern part of it. These slaves constituted a peculiar and powerful interest. All knew that this interest was somehow the cause of the war. To strengthen, perpetuate, and extend this interest was the object for which the insurgents would rend the Union even by war, while the Government claimed no right to do more than to restrict the territorial enlargement of it. Neither party expected for the war the magnitude or the duration which it has already attained. Neither anticipated that the *cause* of the conflict might cease with or even before the conflict itself should cease. Each looked for an easier triumph, and a result less fundamental and astounding. Both read the same Bible and pray to the same God, and each invokes His aid against the other. It may seem strange that any men should dare to ask a just God's assistance in wringing their bread from the sweat of other men's faces, but let us judge not, that we be not judged. The prayers of both could not be answered. That of neither has been answered fully. The Almighty has His own purposes. "Woe unto the world because of offenses; for it must needs be that offenses come, but woe to that man by whom the offense cometh." If we shall suppose that American slavery is one of those offenses which, in the providence of God, must needs come, but which, having continued through His appointed time, He now wills to remove, and that He gives to both North and South this terrible war as the woe due to those by whom the offense came, shall we discern therein any departure from those divine attributes which the believers in a living God always ascribe to Him? Fondly do we hope, fervently do we pray, that this might scourge of war may speedily pass away. Yet, if God wills that it continue until all the wealth piled by the bondman's two hundred and fifty years of unrequited toil shall be sunk, and until every drop of blood drawn with the lash shall be paid by another drawn with the sword, as was said three thousand years ago, so still it must be said, "The judgments of the Lord are true and righteous altogether."

With malice toward none, with charity for all, with firmness in the right as God gives us to see the right, let us strive on to finish the work we are in, to bind up the nation's wounds, to care for him who shall have borne the battle and for his widow and his orphan, to do all which may achieve and cherish a just and lasting peace among ourselves and with all nations.

BLACK CODES
LOCAL REGULATIONS IN LOUISIANA (1865)

The following ordinances are adopted with the approval of the United States military authorities commanding in said parish, viz:

Sec. 1. *Be it ordained by the police jury of the parish of St. Landry*, That no negro shall be allowed to pass within the limits of said parish without special permit in writing from his employer. Whoever shall violate this provision shall pay a fine of two dollars and fifty cents, or in default thereof shall be forced to work four days on the public road, or suffer corporeal punishment as provided hereinafter.

Sec. 2. . . . Every negro who shall be found absent from the residence of his employer after ten o'clock at night, without a written permit from his employer, shall pay a fine of five dollars, or in default thereof, shall be compelled to work five days on the public road, or suffer corporeal punishment as hereinafter provided.

Sec. 3. . . . No negro shall be permitted to rent or keep a house within said parish. Any negro violating this provision shall be immediately ejected and compelled to find an employer; and any person who shall rent, or give the use of any house to any negro, in violation of this section, shall pay a fine of five dollars for each offence.

Sec. 4. . . . Every negro is required to be in the regular service of some white person, or former owner, who shall be held responsible for the conduct of said negro. But said employer or former owner may permit said negro to hire his own time by special permission in writing, which permission shall not extend over seven days at any one time. . . .

Sec. 5. . . . No public meetings or congregations of negroes shall be allowed within said parish after sunset, but such public meetings and congregations may be held between the hours of sunrise and sunset, by the special permission in writing of the captain of patrol, within whose beat such meetings shall take place. This prohibition, however, is not to prevent negroes from attending the usual church services, conducted by white ministers and priests. . . .

Sec. 6. . . . No negro shall be permitted to preach, exhort, or otherwise declaim to congregations of colored people, without a special permission in writing from the president of the police jury. . . .

Sec. 7. . . . No negro who is not in the military service shall be allowed to carry fire-arms, or any kind of weapons, within the parish, without the special written permission of his employers, approved and indorsed by the nearest and most convenient chief of patrol. Any one violating the provisions of this section shall forfeit his weapons and pay a fine of five dollars, or in default of the payment of said fine, shall be forced to work five days on the public road, or suffer corporeal punishment as hereinafter provided.

Sec. 8. . . . No negro shall sell, barter, or exchange any articles of merchandise or traffic within said parish without the special written permission of his employer, specifying the article of sale, barter or traffic. . . .

THE SOUTH MUST BE PUNISHED, 1865
THADDEUS STEVENS

The whole fabric of southern society *must* be changed and never can it be done if this opportunity is lost. Without this, this Government can never be, as it never has been, a true republic. Heretofore, it had more the features of aristocracy than of democracy. -- The Southern States have been despotisms, not governments of the people. It is impossible that any practical equality of rights can exist where a few thousand men monopolize the whole landed property. The larger the number of small proprietors the more safe and stable the government. As the landed interest must govern, the more it is subdivided and held by independent owners, the better. . . . This must be done even though it drive her nobility into exile. If they go, all the better. . . .

When our ancestors found a "more perfect Union" necessary, they found it impossible to agree upon a Constitution without tolerating, nay guaranteeing Slavery. They were obliged to acquiesce, trusting to time to work a speedy cure, in which they were disappointed. *They* had some excuse, some justification. But we can have none if we do not thoroughly eradicate Slavery and render it forever impossible in this republic. The Slave power made war upon the nation. They declared the "more perfect Union" dissolved. Solemnly declared themselves a foreign nation, alien to this republic; for four years were in fact what they claimed to be. We accepted the war which they tendered and treated them as a government capable of making war. We have conquered them, and as a conquered enemy we can give them laws; can abolish all their municipal institutions and form new ones. If we do not make those institutions fit to last through generations of free men, a heavy curse will be on us. Our glorious, but tainted republic, has been born to new life through bloody, agonizing pains. But this frightful "Restoration" has thrown it into "cold obstruction, and to death." If the rebel states have never been out of the Union, any attempt to reform their State institutions either by Congress or the President, is rank usurpation.

THE CIVIL RIGHTS ACT OF 1875
PASSED BY CONGRESS, SIGNED BY PRESIDENT GRANT

Whereas it is essential to just government we recognize the equality of all men before the law, and hold that it is the duty of government in its dealings with the people to mete out equal and exact justice to all, of whatever nativity, race, color, or persuasion, religious or political; and it being the appropriate object of legislation to enact great fundamental principles into law: Therefore,

Be it enacted, That all persons within the jurisdiction of the United States shall be entitled to the full and equal enjoyment of the accommodations, advantages, facilities, and privileges of inns, public conveyances on land or water, theaters, and other places of public amusement; subject only to the conditions and limitations established by law, and applicable alike to citizens of every race and color, regardless of any previous condition of servitude.

Sec. 2. That any person who shall violate the foregoing section by denying to any citizen, except for reasons by law applicable to citizens of every race and color, and regardless of any previous condition of servitude, the full enjoyment of any of the accommodations, advantages, facilities, or privileges in said section enumerated, or by aiding or inciting such denial, shall, for every such offense, forfeit and pay the sum of five hundred dollars to the person aggrieved thereby, . . . and shall also, for every such offense, be deemed guilty of a misdemeanor, and, upon conviction thereof, shall be fined not less than five hundred nor more than one thousand dollars, or shall be imprisoned not less than thirty days nor more than one year. . . .

THE CHINESE EXCLUSION ACT
1882

Be it enacted by the Senate and House of Representatives of the United States of America in Congress assembled, That from and after the expiration of ninety days next after the passage of this act, and until the expiration of ten years next after the passage of this act, the coming of Chinese laborers to the United States be, and the same is hereby, suspended; and during such suspension it shall not be lawful for any Chinese laborer to come, or, having so come after the expiration of said ninety days, to remain within the United States. . . .

Section 14. That hereafter no State court or court of the United States shall admit Chinese to citizenship; and all laws in conflict with this act are hereby repealed.

Excerpts from
"Cheap Labor"
A Chapter from the Report of the
Bureau of Labor Statistics of the State of Connecticut
November 30, 1885

FOREIGN CHEAP LABOR

We are constantly receiving from Europe number of unskilled laborers. At first they are unfamiliar alike with our methods and with our institutions. The employer can hire their labor cheaper. The foreign laborer is in some respects less self-reliant than the American. This gives the employer an advantage in dealing with the individual workmen, but it gives the workmen a greater readiness to combine and, if need be, to strike for the sake of protecting their own interests.

Most of our foreign immigrants soon learn American ways, and adapt themselves to American methods. They are foreigners only while they are learning to become Americans. But there are certain classes of immigrants who do not come to stay. They have no intention of becoming Americans. The most marked instance has been that of the Chinese in California. Of a very different character, but involving some of the same principles, have been the French Canadian immigrants in the Northeast, as well as the stream of immigration from some of the countries of southern and eastern Europe, which is now rapidly setting toward our shores. The Italians are perhaps destined to form a still more perplexing element in other parts of the state.

ITALIANS

The Italian immigrants come almost entirely from the southern districts of Italy. They come in rudely organized bodies; not as a rule under contract from the employers themselves, but under the leadership of certain of their own nation, who arrange concerning their employment and pay. The Italian's object in coming to this country is simple. He wishes to stay here until he can save two or three hundred dollars, and then go home again. This sum amounts to a competence in his own country, and enables him to pass the remainder of his days as a man of wealth and established position. Staying here for the short time that he does, the Italian has little or no inducement to learn English, and still less to change his habits or methods of living.

The task which he has before him is not a hard one. He has many advantages as a laborer. He is not quite so industrious as the French Canadian; but the desire to earn money gives him an active enough stimulus in that respect. He is usually quite strong, and almost always handy and quick to learn. When employed in out-door work he has no difficulty in getting from a dollar and a quarter to a dollar and a half a day for his services. His expenses he is able to reduce to a minimum. In matters of personal comfort he is the reverse of exacting. He can bear an infinite amount of crowding, without apparently interfering with his enjoyment of life or his sense of decency.

. . . The food of the Italian consists largely of stale bread, stale fruit, and stale beer. The Italians use these things at a point where they have ceased to be marketable. Of fruit in particular they save large quantities at a point where it has almost no commercial value, applying a kind of drying process of their own, and afterwards cooking the dried fruit from time to time as it is wanted. We have no accurate means of measuring their expenses, but, judging by the standard attained, they must be exceedingly small. Working in this way, and living in this way, they are able to compete successfully with American labor, and to accomplish the objects for which they come, within a very short space of time. If the Italian immigration into Connecticut continues to increase in the next five years as it has done in the past five years, it is certain to become almost perplexing social problem, what effect it will have on our native unskilled labor. Whenever a race with equal capacity and fewer wants comes in to compete with our unskilled laborers already on the ground, it means one of two things: Rise, or die. Some will rise and some will die. If we give no legislative protection at all we may find ourselves swamped with foreigners. If we try too much legislative protection we do a great deal to destroy self-reliance and enterprise. It will not do to look at either alternative exclusively.

POPULIST PARTY PLATFORM, 1892
PREAMBLE

The conditions which surround us best justify our cooperation; we meet in the midst of a nation brought to the verge of moral, political, and material ruin. Corruption dominates the ballot-box, the legislatures, the Congress, and touches even the ermine of the bench. The people are demoralized; most of the States have been compelled to isolate the voters at the polling places to prevent universal intimidation and bribery. The newspapers are largely subsidized or muzzled, public opinion silenced, business prostrated, homes covered with mortgages, labor impoverished, and the land concentrated in the hands of capitalists. The urban workmen are denied the right to organize for self-protection, imported pauperized labor beats down their wages, a hireling standing army, unrecognized by our laws, is established to shoot them down, and they are rapidly degenerating into European conditions. The fruits of the toil of millions are boldly stolen to build up colossal fortunes for a few, unprecedented in the history of mankind; and the possessors of those, in turn, despise the Republic and endanger liberty. From the same prolific womb of governmental injustice we breed the two great classes -- tramps and millionaires.

We have witnessed for more than a quarter of a century the struggles of the two great political parties for power and plunder, while grievous wrongs have been inflicted upon the suffering people. We charge that the controlling influences dominating both these parties have permitted the existing dreadful conditions to develop without serious effort to prevent or restrain them. Neither do they now promise us any substantial reform. They have agreed together to ignore, in the coming campaign, every issue but one. They propose to drown the outcries of a plundered people with the uproar of a sham battle over the tariff, so that capitalists, corporations, national banks, rings, trusts, watered stock, the demonetization of silver and the oppressions of the usurers may all be lost sight of. They propose to sacrifice our homes, lives, and children on the alter of mammon; to destroy the multitude in order to secure corruption funds from the millionaires.

We believe that the power of government -- in other words, of the people -- should be expanded (as in the case of the postal service) as rapidly and as far as the good sense of an intelligent people and the teachings of experience shall justify, to the end that oppression, injustice, and poverty shall eventually cease in the land.

PLATFORM

We declare, therefore:

We believe that the time has come when the railroad corporations will either own the people or the people must own the railroads, and should the Government enter upon the work of owning and managing all roads, we should favor an amendment to the Constitution by which all persons engaged in the Government service shall be placed under a civil service regulation of the most rigid character, so as to prevent the increase of the power of the national administration by the use of such additional Government employees.

1. We demand free and unlimited coinage of silver and gold at the present legal ratio of 16 to 1.

3. We demand a graduated income tax.

4. We believe that the money of the country should be kept as much as possible in the hands of the people, and hence we demand that all State and national revenues shall be limited to the necessary expenses of the Government, economically and honestly administered.

EXPRESSION OF SENTIMENTS

WHEREAS, Other questions have been presented for our consideration, we hereby submit the following, not as a part of the Platform of the People's Party, but as resolutions expressive of the sentiment of this Convention:

1. *Resolved*, That we demand a free ballot and a fair grant in all elections, and pledge ourselves to secure it to every legal voter without Federal intervention, through the adoption by the States of the unperverted Australian or secret ballot system.

4. *Resolved*, That we condemn the fallacy of protecting American labor under the present system, which opens our ports to the pauper and criminal classes of the world and crowds out our wage-earners; and we denounce the present ineffective laws against contract labor, and demand the further restriction of undesirable emigration.

5. *Resolved*, That we cordially sympathize with the efforts of organized workingmen to shorten the hours of labor, and demand a rigid enforcement of the existing eight-hour law on Government work, and ask that a penalty clause be added to the said law.

8. *Resolved*, That we favor a constitutional provision limiting the office of President and Vice-President to one term, and providing for the election of Senators of the United States by a direct vote of the people.

PLESSY v. FERGUSON
1896

The constitutionality of this act is attacked upon the ground that it conflicts both with the 13th Amendment of the Constitution, abolishing slavery, and the 14th Amendment, which prohibits certain restrictive legislation on the part of the states.

1. That it does not conflict with the 13th Amendment, which abolished slavery and involuntary servitude, except as a punishment for crime, is too clear for argument. . . .

The object of the 14th Amendment was undoubtedly to enforce the absolute equality of the two races before the law, but in the nature of things it could not have been intended to abolish distinctions based upon color, or to enforce social, as distinguished from political, equality, or a commingling of the two races upon terms unsatisfactory to either. Laws permitting, and even requiring their separation in places where they are liable to be brought into contact do not necessarily imply the inferiority of either race to the other, and have been generally, if not universally, recognized as within the competency of the state legislatures in the exercise of their police power. The most common instance of this connected with the establishment of separate schools for white and colored children, which have been held to be a valid exercise of the legislative power even by courts of states where the political rights of the colored race have been longest and most earnestly enforced. . .

We consider the underlying fallacy of the plaintiff's argument to consist in the assumption that the enforced separation of the two races stamps the colored race with a badge of inferiority. If this be so, it is not by reason of anything found in the act, but solely because the colored race chooses to put that construction upon it. The argument necessarily assumes that if, as has been more than once the case, and is not unlikely to be so again, the colored race should become the dominant power in the state legislature, and should enact a law in precisely similar terms, it would thereby relegate the white race to an inferior position. We imagine that the white race, at least, would not acquiesce in this assumption. The argument also assumes that social prejudice may be overcome by legislation, and that equal rights cannot be secured to the Negro except by an enforced commingling of the two races. We cannot accept this proposition. If the two races are to meet on terms of social equality, it must be the result of natural affinities, a mutual appreciation of each other's merits and a voluntary consent of individuals. . . . Legislation is powerless to eradicate racial instincts or to abolish distinctions based upon physical differences, and the attempt to do so can only result in accentuating the difficulties of the present situation. If the civil and political right of both races be equal, one cannot be inferior to the other civilly or politically. If one race be inferior to the other socially, the Constitution of the United States cannot put them upon the same plane.

Justice Harlan, dissenting. . . . In respect of civil rights, common to all citizens, the Constitution of the United States does not, I think, permit any public authority to know the race of those entitled to be protected in the enjoyment of such rights. Every true man has pride of race, and under appropriate circumstances, when the rights of others, his equals before the law, are not to be affected, it is his privilege to express such pride and to take such action based upon it as to him seems proper. But I deny that any legislative body or judicial tribunal may have regard to the race of citizens when the civil rights of those citizens are involved. Indeed such legislation as that here in question is inconsistent, not only with that equality of rights which pertains to citizenship, national and state, but with the personal liberty enjoyed by every one within the United States. . . .

In my opinion, the judgment this day rendered will, in time, prove to be quite as pernicious as the decision made by this tribunal in the Dred Scott Case. It was adjudged in that case that the descendants of Africans who were imported into this country and sold as slaves were not included nor intended to be included under the word "citizens" in the Constitution, and could not claim any of the rights and privileges which that instrument provided for and secured to citizens of the United States; that at the time of the adoption of the Constitution they were "considered as a subordinate and inferior class of beings, who had been subjugated by the dominant race, and, whether emancipated or not, yet remained subject to their authority, and had no rights or privileges but such as those who held the power and the government might choose to grant them." The recent amendments of the Constitution, it was supposed, had eradicated these principles from our institutions. But it seems that we have yet, in some of the states, a dominant race, a superior class of citizens, which assumes to regulate the enjoyment of civil rights, common to all citizens, upon the basis of race. The present decision, it may well be apprehended, will not only stimulate aggressions, more or less brutal and irritating, upon the admitted rights of colored citizens, but will encourage the belief that it is possible, by means of state enactments, to defeat the beneficent purposes which the people of the United States had in view when they adopted the recent amendments of the Constitution, by one of which the blacks of this country were made citizens of the United States and of the states in which they respectively reside and whose privileges and immunities, as citizens, the states are forbidden to abridge. Sixty millions of whites are in not danger from the presence here of eight millions of blacks. The destinies of the two races in this country are indissolubly linked together, and the interest of both require that the common government of all shall not permit the seeds of race hate to be planted under the sanction of law. What can more certainly arouse race hate, what more certainly create and perpetuate a feeling of distrust between these races, than state enactments which in fact proceed on the ground that colored citizens are so inferior and degraded that they cannot be allowed to sit in public coaches occupied by white citizens? That, as all will admit, is the real meaning of such legislation as was enacted in Louisiana. . . .

If evils will result from the commingling of the two races upon public highways established for the benefit of all, they will be infinitely less than those that will surely come from state legislation regulating the enjoyment of civil rights upon the basis of race. We boast of the freedom enjoyed by our people above all other peoples. But it is difficult to reconcile that boast with a state of the law which, practically, puts the brand of servitude and degradation upon a large class of our fellow citizens, our equals before the law. The thin disguise of "equal" accommodations for passengers in railroad coaches will not mislead anyone, or atone for the wrong this day done. . . .

I am of opinion that the statute of Louisiana is inconsistent with the personal liberty of citizens, white and black, in that state, and hostile to both the spirit and letter of the Constitution of the United States. If laws of like character should be enacted in the several states of the Union, the effect would be in the highest degree mischievous. Slavery as an institution tolerated by law would, it is true, have disappeared from our country, but there would remain a power in the states, by sinister legislation, to interfere with the full enjoyment of the blessings of freedom; to regulate civil rights, common to all citizens, upon the basis of race; and to place in a condition of legal inferiority a large body of American citizens, now constituting a part of the political community, called the people of the Untied States, for whom and by whom, through representatives, our government is administered. Such a system is inconsistent with the guarantee given by the Constitution to each state of a republican form of government, and may be stricken down by Congressional action, or by the courts in the discharge of their solemn duty to maintain the supreme law of the land, anything in the Constitution or laws of any state to the contrary notwithstanding.

For the reasons stated, I am constrained to withhold my assent from the opinion and judgment of the majority.　　　　　Vote 8-1

WILLIAM MCKINLEY'S WAR MESSAGE AGAINST SPAIN
1898

The present revolution is but the successor of other similar insurrections which have occurred in Cuba against the dominion of Spain, extending over a period of nearly half a century, each of which during its progress has subjected the United States to great effort and expense in enforcing its neutrality laws, caused enormous losses to American trade and commerce, caused irritation, annoyance, and disturbance among our citizens, and, by the exercise of cruel, barbarous, and uncivilized practices of warfare, shocked the sensibilities and offended the humane sympathies of our people....

Our trade has suffered, the capital invested by our citizens in Cuba has been largely lost, and the temper and forbearance of our people have been so sorely tried as to beget a perilous unrest among our own citizens, which has inevitably found its expression from time to time in the National Legislature, so that issues wholly external to our own body politic engross attention and stand in the way of that close devotion to domestic advancement that becomes a self-contained commonwealth whose primal maxim has been the avoidance of all foreign entanglements. All this must need awaken, and has, indeed, aroused, the utmost concern on the part of this Government, as well during my predecessor's term as in my own. . . .

The grounds for . . . intervention may be briefly summarized as follows:

First. In the cause of humanity and to put an end to barbarities, bloodshed, starvation, and horrible miseries now existing there, and which the parties to the conflict are either unable or unwilling to stop or mitigate. It is no answer to say this is all in another country, belonging to another nation, and is therefore none of our business. It is specially our duty, for it is right at our door.

Second. We owe it to our citizens in Cuba to afford them that protection and indemnity for life and property which no government there can or will afford, and to that end to terminate the conditions that deprive them of legal protection.

Third. The right to intervene may be justified by the very serious injury to the commerce, trade, and business of our people and by the wanton destruction of property and devastation of the island.

Fourth, and which is of the utmost importance. The present condition of affairs in Cuba is a constant menace to our peace and entails upon this Government an enormous expense. With such a conflict waged for years in an island so near us and with which our people have such trade and business relations; when the lives and liberty of our citizens are in constant danger and their property destroyed and themselves ruined; where our trading vessels are liable to seizure and are seized at our very door by war ships of a foreign nation.

The naval court of inquiry, which, . . . was unanimous in its conclusion that the destruction of the <u>Maine</u> was caused by an exterior explosion--that of a submarine mine. It did not assume to place the responsibility. That remains to be fixed.

...I ask the Congress to authorize and empower the President to take measures to secure a full and final termination of hostilities between the government of Spain and the people of Cuba...and to use the military and naval forces of the United States...

THE ROOSEVELT COROLLARY TO THE MONROE DOCTRINE

Roosevelt's Annual Message to Congress
December 6, 1904

All that this country desires is to see the neighboring countries stable, orderly, and prosperous. Any country whose people conduct themselves well can count upon our hearty friendship. If a nation shows that it knows how to act with reasonable efficiency and decency in social and political matters, if it keeps order and pays its obligations, it need fear no interference from the United States. Chronic wrong doing, or an impotence which results in a general loosening of the ties of civilized society, may in America, as elsewhere, ultimately require intervention by some civilized nation, and in the Western Hemisphere the adherence of the United States to the Monroe Doctrine may force the United States, however reluctantly, in flagrant cases of such wrong doing or impotence, to the exercise of an international police power. Our interests and those of our southern neighbors are in reality identical. They have great natural riches, and if within their borders the reign of law and justice obtains, prosperity is sure to come to them. While they thus obey the primary laws of civilized society they may rest assured that they will be treated by us in a spirit of cordial and helpful sympathy. We would interfere with them only in the last resort, and then only if it became evident that their inability or unwillingness to do justice at home and abroad had violated the rights of the United States or had invited foreign aggression to the detriment of the entire body of American nations.

We are in the presence of a new organization of society. Our life has broken away from the past. The life of America is not the life that it was twenty years ago; it is not the life that it was ten years ago. We have changed our economic conditions, absolutely, from top to bottom; and, with our economic society, the organization of our life. The old political formulas do not fit the present problems; they read now like documents taken out of a forgotten age. The older cries sound as if they belonged to a past age which men have almost forgotten. Things which used to be put into the party platforms of ten years ago would sound antiquated if put into a platform now. We are facing the necessity of fitting a new social organization, as we did once fit the old organization, to the happiness and prosperity of the great body of citizens; for we are conscious that the new order of society has not been made to fit and provide the convenience or prosperity of the average man.

We have come upon a very different age from any that preceded us. We have come upon an age when we do not do business in the way in which we used to do business,--when we do not carry on any of the operations of manufacture, sale, transportation, or communication as men used to carry them on. There is a sense in which in our day the individual has been submerged. In most parts of our country men work, not for themselves, not a partners in the old way in which they used to work, but generally as employees,--in a higher or lower grade,--of great corporations. There was a time when corporations played a very minor part in our business affairs, but now they play the chief part, and most men are the servants of corporations...

So what we have to discuss is, not wrongs which individuals intentionally do,--I do not believe there are a great many of those,--but the wrongs of a system. I want to record my protest against any discussion of this matter which would seem to indicate that there are bodies of our fellow citizens who are trying to grind us down and do us injustice. There are some men of that sort. I don't know how they sleep o' nights, but there are men of that kind. Thank God, they are not numerous. The truth is, we are all caught in a great economic system which is heartless. The modern corporation is not engaged in business as an individual...

What this country needs above everything else is a body of laws which will look after the men who are on the make rather than the men who are already made. Because the men who are already made are not going to live indefinitely, and they are not always kind enough to leave sons as able and as honest as they are...

The originative part of America, the part of America that makes new enterprises, the part into which the ambitious and gifted workingman makes his way up, the class that saves, that plans, that organizes, that presently spreads its enterprises until they have a national scope and character,--that middle class is being more and more squeezed out by the processes which we have been taught to call processes of prosperity. Its members are sharing prosperity, no doubt; but what alarms me is that they are not *originating* prosperity. No country can afford to have its prosperity originated by a small controlling class. The treasury of America does not lie in the brains of the small body of men now in control of the great enterprises that have been concentrated under the direction of a very small number of persons. The treasury of America lies in those ambitions, those energies, that cannot be restricted to a special favored class. It depends upon the inventions of unknown men, upon the originations of unknown men, upon the ambitions of unknown men. Every country is renewed out of the ranks of the unknown, not out of the ranks of those already famous and powerful and in control.

There has come over the land that un-American set of conditions which enable a small number of men who control the government to get favors from the government; by those favors to exclude their fellows from equal business opportunity; by those favors to extend a network of control that will presently dominate every industry in the country...

One of the most alarming phenomena of the time,--or rather it would be alarming if the nation had not awakened to it and shown its determination to control it,--one of the most significant signs of the new social era is the degree to which government has become associated with business. I speak, for the moment, of the control over the government exercised by Big Business. Behind the whole subject, of course, is the truth that, in the new order, government and business must be associated closely. But that association is at present of a nature absolutely intolerable; the precedence is wrong; the association is upside down. Our government has been for the past few years under the control of heads of great allied corporations with special interests. It has not controlled these interests and assigned them a proper place in the whole system of business; it has submitted itself to their control. As a result, there have grown up vicious systems and schemes of governmental favoritism (the most obvious being the extravagant tariff), far-reaching in effect upon the whole fabric of life, touching to his injury every inhabitant of the land, laying unfair and impossible handicaps upon competitors, imposing taxes in every direction, stifling everywhere the free spirit of American enterprise...

We stand in the presence of a revolution,--not a bloody revolution; America is not given to the spilling of blood,--but a silent revolution, whereby America will insist upon recovering in practice those ideals which she has always professed, upon securing a government devoted to the general interest and not to special interests.

WOODROW WILSON ON NEUTRALITY, 1914

The effect of the war upon the United States will depend upon what American citizens say and do. Every man who really loves America will act and speak in the true spirit of neutrality, which is the spirit of impartiality and fairness and friendliness to all concerned.

The people of the United States are drawn from many nations, and chiefly from the nations now at war. It is natural and inevitable that there should be the utmost variety of sympathy and desire among them with regard to the issues and circumstances of the conflict. Some will wish one nation, others another, to succeed in the momentous struggle.

Such divisions among us would be fatal to our peace of mind and might seriously stand in the way of the proper performance of our duty as the one great nation at peace, the one people holding itself ready to play a part of impartial mediation and speak the counsels of peace and accommodation, not as a partisan, but as a friend.

The United States must be neutral in fact as well as in name during these days that are to try men's souls. We must be impartial in thought as well as in action, must put a curb upon our sentiments as well as upon every transaction that might be construed as a preference of one party to the struggle before another.

My thought is of America. I am speaking, I feel sure, the earnest wish and purpose of every thoughtful American that this great country of ours, which is, of course, the first in our thoughts and in our hearts, should show herself in this time of peculiar trial a Nation fit beyond others to exhibit the fine poise of undisturbed judgment, the dignity of self-control, the efficiency of dispassionate action; a Nation that neither sits in judgment upon others nor is disturbed in her own counsels and which keeps herself fit and free to do what is honest and disinterested and truly serviceable for the peace of the world.

Shall we not resolve to put upon ourselves the restraints which will bring to our people the happiness and the great and lasting influence for peace we covet for them?

HERBERT HOOVER AND AMERICAN VALUES
October 22, 1928

After the war, when the Republican Party assumed administration of the country, we were faced with the problem of determination of the very nature of our national life. During one hundred and fifty years we have builded up a form of self-government and have a social system which is peculiarly our own. It differs essentially from all others in the world. It is the American system. It is just as definite and positive a political and social system as has ever been developed on earth. It is founded upon a particular conception of self-government in which decentralized local responsibility is the very base. Further than this, it is founded upon the conception that only through ordered liberty, freedom, and equal opportunity to the individual will his initiative and enterprise spur on the march of progress. And in our insistence upon equality of opportunity has our system advanced beyond all the world.

During the war we necessarily turned to the Government to solve every difficult economic problem. The Government having absorbed every energy of our people for war, there was no other solution. For the preservation of the State the Federal Government became a centralized despotism which undertook unprecedented responsibilities, assumed autocratic powers, and took over the business of citizens. To a large degree we regimented our whole people temporarily into a socialistic state. However justified in time of war, if continued in peace-time it would destroy not only our American system but with it our progress and freedom as well.

When the war closed, the most vital of all issues both in our own country and throughout the world was whether governments should continue their wartime ownership and operation of many instrumentalities of production and distribution. We were challenged with a peace-time choice between the American system of rugged individualism and a European philosophy of diametrically opposed doctrines--doctrines of paternalism and state socialism. The acceptance of these ideas would have meant the destruction of self-government through centralization of government. It would have meant the undermining of the individual initiative and enterprise through which our people have grown to unparalleled greatness. . . .

It is a false liberalism that interprets itself into the Government operation of commercial business. Every step of bureaucratizing of the business of our country poisons the very roots of liberalism--that is, political equality, free speech, free assembly, free press, and equality of opportunity. It is the road not to more liberty, but to less liberty. Liberalism should be found not striving to spread bureaucracy but striving to set bounds to it. True liberalism seeks all legitimate freedom first in the confident belief that without such freedom the pursuit of all other blessings and benefits is vain. That belief is the foundation of all American progress, political as well as economic.

Liberalism is a force truly of the spirit, a force preceding from the deep realization that economic freedom cannot be sacrificed if political freedom is to be preserved. Even if Governmental conduct of business could give us more efficiency instead of less efficiency, the fundamental objection to it would remain unaltered and unabated. It would destroy political equality. It would increase rather than decrease abuse and corruption. It would stifle initiative and invention. It would undermine the development of leadership. It would cramp and cripple the mental and spiritual energies of our people. It would extinguish equality and opportunity. It would dry up the sprit of liberty and progress. For these reasons primarily it must be resisted. For a hundred and fifty years liberalism has found its true spirit in the American system, not in the European system.

I do not wish to be misunderstood in this statement. I am defining a general policy. It does not mean that our Government is to part with one iota of its national resources without complete protection to the public interest. . . .

Nor do I wish to be misinterpreted as believing that the United States is free-for-all and devil-take-the-hindmost. The very essence of equality of opportunity and of American individualism is that there shall be no domination by any group or combination in this Republic, whether it be business or political. On the contrary, it demands economic justice as well as political and social justice. It is no system of laissez faire. . . .

By adherence to the principles of decentralized self-government, ordered liberty, equal opportunity, and freedom to the individual, our American experiment in human welfare has yielded a degree of well-being unparalleled in all the world. It has come nearer to the abolition of poverty, to the abolition of fear of want, than humanity has ever reached before. . . I again repeat that the departure from our American system by injecting principles destructive to it which our opponents propose, will jeopardize the very liberty and freedom of our people, and will destroy equality of opportunity not alone to ourselves but to our children. . . .

FRANKLIN D. ROOSEVELT'S FIRST INAUGURAL ADDRESS
(1933)

President Hoover, Mr. Chief Justice, my friends:

This is a day of national consecration, and I am certain that my fellow Americans expect that on my induction into the Presidency I will address them with a candor and a decision which the present situation of our nation impels.

This is pre-eminently the time to speak the truth, the whole truth, frankly and boldly. Nor need we shrink from honestly facing conditions in our country today. This great nation will endure as it has endured, will revive and will prosper.

So first of all let me assert my firm belief that the only thing we have to fear is fear itself--nameless, unreasoning, unjustified terror which paralyzes needed efforts to convert retreat into advance.

In every dark hour of our national life a leadership of frankness and vigor has met with that understanding and support of the people themselves which is essential to victory. I am convinced that you will again give that support to leadership in these critical days.

In such a spirit on my part and on yours we face our common difficulties. They concern, thank God, only material things. Values have shrunken to fantastic levels; taxes have risen; our ability to pay has fallen, government of all kinds is faced by serious curtailment of income; the means of exchange are frozen in the currents of trade; the withered leaves of industrial enterprise lie on every side; farmers find no markets for their produce; the savings of many years in thousands of families are gone.

More important, a host of unemployed citizens face the grim problem of existence, and an equally great number toil with little return. Only a foolish optimist can deny the dark realities of the moment.

Yet our distress comes from no failure of substance. We are stricken by no plague of locusts. Compared with the perils which our forefathers conquered because they believed and were not afraid, we have still much to be thankful for. Nature still offers her bounty and human efforts have multiplied it. Plenty is at our doorstop, but a generous use of it languishes in the very sight of the supply.

Primarily, this is because the rulers of the exchange of mankind's goods have failed through their own stubbornness and their own incompetence, have admitted their failure and abdicated. Practices of the unscrupulous money changers stand indicted in the court of public opinion, rejected by the hearts and minds of men.

...The money changers have fled from their high seats in the temple of our civilization. We may now restore that temple to the ancient truths.

The measure of the restoration lies in the extent to which we apply social values more noble than mere monetary profit.

Happiness lies not in the mere possession of money; it likes in the joy of achievement, in the thrill of creative effort.

The joy and moral stimulation of work no longer must be forgotten in the mad chase of evanescent profits. These dark days will be worth all they cost us if they teach us that our true destiny is not to be ministered unto but to minister to ourselves and to our fellow men.

Recognition of the falsity of material wealth as the standard of success goes hand in hand with the abandonment of the false belief that public office and high political position are to be valued only by the standards of pride of place and personal profit; and there must be an end to a conduct in banking and in business which too often has given to a sacred trust the likeness of callous and selfish wrongdoing.

Small wonder that confidence languishes, for it thrives only on honesty, on honor, on the sacredness of obligations, on faithful protection, on unselfish performance. Without them it cannot live.

Restoration calls, however, not for changes in ethics alone. This nation asks for action, and action now.

Our greatest primary task is to put people to work. This is not unsolvable problem if we face it wisely and courageously.

It can be accomplished in part by direct recruiting by the government itself, treating the task as we would treat the emergency of a war, but at the same time, through this employment, accomplishing greatly needed projects to stimulate and reorganize the use of our natural resources.

Hand in hand with this, we must frankly recognize the overbalance of population in our industrial centers and, by engaging on a national scale in the redistribution, endeavor to provide a better use of the land for those best fitted for the land.

The task can be helped by definite efforts to raise the values of agricultural products and with this the power to purchase the output of our cities.

It can be helped by preventing realistically the tragedy of the growing loss, through foreclosure, of our small homes and our farms.

It can be helped by insistence that the Federal, State and local governments act forthwith on the demand that their cost be drastically reduced.

It can be helped by the unifying of relief activities which today are often scattered, uneconomical and unequal. It can be helped by national planning for and supervision of all forms of transportation and of communications and other utilities which have a definitely public character.

There are many ways in which it can be helped, but it can never be helped merely by talking about it. We must act, and act quickly.

Finally, in our progress toward a resumption of work we require two safeguards against a return of the evils of the old order; there must be a strict supervision of all banking and credits and investments; there must be an end to speculation with other people's money, and there must be provision for an adequate but sound currency.

There are the lines of attack. I shall presently urge upon a new Congress in special session detailed measures for their fulfillment, and I shall seek the immediate assistance of the several States.

Through this program of action we address ourselves to putting our own national house in order and making income balance outgo.

Our international trade relations, though vastly important, are, in point of time and necessity, secondary to the establishment of a sound national economy.

I favor as a practical policy the putting of first things first. I shall spare no effort to restore world trade by international economic readjustment, but the emergency at home cannot wait on that accomplishment.

The basic thought that guides these specific means of national recovery is not narrowly nationalistic.

It is the insistence, as a first consideration, upon the interdependence of the various elements in, and parts of, the United States--a recognition of the old and permanently important manifestation of the American spirit of the pioneer.

It is the way to recovery. It is the immediate way. It is the strongest assurance that the recovery will endure.

In the field of world policy I would dedicate this nation to the policy of the good neighbor--the neighbor who resolutely respects himself and, because he does so, respects the rights of others--the neighbor who respects his obligations and respects the sanctity of his agreements in and with a world of neighbors.

If I read the temper of our people correctly, we now realize as we have never before, our interdependence on each other; that we cannot merely take, but we must give as well; that if we are to go forward we must move as a trained and loyal army willing to sacrifice for the good of a common discipline, because, without such discipline, no progress is made, no leadership becomes effective.

...Action in this image and to this end is feasible under the form of government which we have inherited from our ancestors.

Our Constitution is so simple and practical that it is possible always to meet extraordinary needs by changes in emphasis and arrangement without loss of essential form.

That is why our constitutional system has proved itself the most superbly enduring political mechanism the modern world has produced. It has met every stress of vast expansion of territory, of foreign wars, of bitter internal strife, of world relations.

It is to be hoped that the normal balance of executive and legislative authority may be wholly adequate to meet the unprecedented task before us. But it may be that an unprecedented demand and need for undelayed action may call for temporary departure from that normal balance of public procedure.

I am prepared under my constitutional duty to recommend the measures that a stricken nation in the midst of a stricken world may require.

These measures, or such other measures as the Congress may build out of its experience and wisdom, I shall seek, within my constitutional authority, to bring to speedy adoption.

But in the event that the Congress shall fail to take one of these two courses, and in the event the national emergency is still critical, I shall not evade the clear course of duty that will then confront me.

I shall ask the Congress for the one remaining instrument to meet the crisis--broad executive power to wage a war against the emergency as great as the power that would be given me if we were in fact invaded by a foreign foe. . . .

We face the arduous days that lie before us in the warm courage of national unity; with the clear consciousness of seeking old and precious moral values; with the clean satisfaction that comes from the stern performance of duty by old and young alike.

We aim at the assurance of a rounded and permanent national life.

We do not distrust the future of essential democracy. The people of the United States have not failed. In their need they have registered a mandate that they want direct, vigorous action.

They have asked for discipline and direction under leadership. They have made me the present instrument of their wishes. In the spirit of the gift I take it.

In this dedication of a nation we humbly ask the blessing of God. May He protect each and every one of us! May He guide me in the days to come!

FRANKLIN D. ROOSEVELT'S "FOUR FREEDOMS" SPEECH
JANUARY 6, 1941

Every realist knows that the democratic way of life is at this moment being directly assailed in every part of the world--assailed either by arms, or by secret spreading of poisonous propaganda by those who seek to destroy unity and promote discord in nations that are still at peace.

Therefore, as your President, performing my constitutional duty to "give to the Congress information of the state of the Union," I find it, unhappily, necessary to report that the future and the safety of our country and of our democracy are overwhelmingly involved in events far beyond our borders.

I have recently pointed out how quickly the tempo of modern warfare could bring into our very midst the physical attack which we must eventually expect if the dictator nations win this war.

As long as the aggressor nations maintain the offensive, they--not we-- will choose the time and the place and the method of their attack.

That is why the future of all the American Republics is today in serious danger.

That is why this Annual Message to the Congress is unique in our history...

Just as our national policy in internal affairs has been based upon a decent respect for the rights and the dignity of all our fellow men within our gates, so our national policy in foreign affairs has been based on a decent respect for the rights and dignity of all nations, large and small. And the justice of morality must and will win in the end.

Our national policy is this:

First, by an impressive expression of the public will and without regard to partisanship, we are committed to all-inclusive national defense.

Second, by an impressive expression of the public will and without regard to partisanship, we are committed to the proposition that principles of morality and considerations for our own security will never permit us to acquiesce in a peace dictated by aggressors and sponsored by appeasers.

Our most useful and immediate role is to act as an arsenal for them as well as for ourselves. They do not need man power, but they do need billions of dollars worth of the weapons of defense.

The time is near when they will not be able to pay for them all in ready cash. We cannot, and we will not, tell them that they must surrender, merely because of inability to pay for the weapons which we know they must have.

I do not recommend that we make them a loan of dollars with which to pay for these weapons--a loan to be repaid in dollars.

I recommend that we make it possible for those nations to continue to obtain war materials in the United States, fitting their orders into our own program. Nearly all their material would, if the time ever came, be useful for our own defense.

Let us say to the democracies: "We Americans are vitally concerned in your defense of freedom. We are putting forth our energies, our resources and our organizing powers to give you the strength to regain and maintain a free world. We shall send you, in ever-increasing numbers, ships, planes, tanks, guns. This is our purpose and our pledge."

In the future days, which we seek to make secure, we look forward to a world founded upon four essential human freedoms.

The first is freedom of speech and expression--everywhere in the world.

The second is freedom of every person to worship God in his own way-everywhere in the world.

The third is freedom from want--which, translated into world terms, means economic understandings which will secure to every nation a healthy peacetime life for its inhabitants--everywhere in the world.

The fourth is freedom from fear--which, translated into world terms, means economic understandings which will secure to every nation a healthy peacetime life for its inhabitants--everywhere in the world.

The fourth is freedom from fear--which, translated into world terms, means a world-wide reduction of armaments to such a point and in such a thorough fashion that no nation will be in a position to commit an act of physical aggression against any neighbor--anywhere in the world.

FRANKLIN D. ROOSEVELT'S WAR MESSAGE AGAINST JAPAN, 1941

Yesterday, December 7, 1941--a date which will live in infamy--the United States of America was suddenly and deliberately attacked by naval and air forces of the empire of Japan.

The United States was at peace with that nation and, at the solicitation of Japan, was still in conversation with its government and its emperor looking toward the maintenance of peace in the Pacific.

Indeed, one hour after Japanese air squadrons had commenced bombing in the American Island of Oahu, the Japanese Ambassador to the United States and his colleague delivered to our Secretary of State a formal reply to a recent American message. And, while this reply stated that it seemed useless to continue the existing diplomatic negotiations, it contained no threat or hint of war or of armed attack.

It will be recorded that the distance of Hawaii from Japan makes it obvious that the attack was deliberately planned many days or even weeks ago. During the intervening time the Japanese Government has deliberately sought to deceive the United States by false statements and expressions of hope for continued peace.

The attack yesterday on the Hawaiian Islands has caused severe damage to American naval and military forces. I regret to tell you that very many Americans lives have been lost. In addition American ships have been reported torpedoed on the high seas between San Francisco and Honolulu.

Yesterday the Japanese Government also launched an attack against Malaya.

Last night Japanese forces attacked Hong Kong.

Last night Japanese forces attacked Guam.

Last night Japanese forces attacked the Philippine Islands.

Last night the Japanese forces attacked Wake Island.

And this morning the Japanese attached Midway Island.

Japan has therefore undertaken a surprise offensive extending throughout the Pacific area. The facts of yesterday and today speak for themselves. The people of the United States have already formed their opinions and well understand the implications to the very life and safety of our nation.

As Commander in Chief of the Army and Navy I have directed that all measures be taken for our defense.

Always will our whole nation remember the character of the onslaught against us.

No matter how long it may take us to overcome this premeditated invasion, the American people, in their righteous might, will win through to absolute victory.

I believe that I interpret the will of the Congress and of the people when I assert that we will not only defend ourselves to the uttermost but will make it very certain that this form of treachery shall never again endanger us.

Hostilities exist. There is no blinking at the fact that our people, our territory and our interests are in grave danger.

With confidence in our armed forces, with the unbounding determination of our people, we will gain the inevitable triumph. So help us God.

I ask that the Congress declare that since the unprovoked and dastardly attack by Japan on Sunday, December 7, 1941, a state of war has existed between the United States and the Japanese Empire.

THE TRUMAN DOCTRINE
March 12, 1947

The gravity of the situation which confronts the world today necessitates my appearance before a joint session of the Congress.

The foreign policy and the national security of this country are involved.

One aspect of the present situation, which I wish to present to you at this time for your consideration and decision, concerns Greece and Turkey.

The United States has received from the Greek government an urgent appeal for financial and economic assistance. Preliminary reports from the American economic mission now in Greece and reports from the American Ambassador in Greece corroborate the statement of the Greek government that assistance is imperative if Greece is to survive as a free nation. . . .

Greece is today without funds to finance the importation of those goods which are essential to bare subsistence. Under these circumstances the people of Greece cannot make progress in solving their problems of reconstruction. Greece is in desperate need of financial and economic assistance to enable it to resume purchases of food, clothing, fuel and seeds. These are indispensable for the subsistence of its people and are obtainable only from abroad. Greece must have help to import the goods necessary to restore internal order and security so essential for economic and political recovery.

The Greek government has also asked for the assistance of experienced American administrators, economists and technicians to insure that the financial and other aid given to Greece shall be used effectively in creating a stable and self-sustaining economy and in improving its public administration.

The very existence of the Greek state is today threatened by the terrorist activities of several thousand armed men, led by Communists, who defy the government's authority at a number of points, particularly along the northern boundaries. A commission appointed by the United Nations Security Council is at present investigating disturbed conditions in northern Greece on the one hand and Albania, Bulgaria and Yugoslavia on the other.

Meanwhile, the Greek government is unable to cope with the situation. The Greek army is small and poorly equipped. It needs supplies and equipment if it is to restore the authority of the government throughout Greek territory.

Greece must have assistance if it is to become a self-supporting and self-respecting democracy.

The United States must supply that assistance. We have already extended to Greece certain types of relief and economic aid but these are inadequate.

There is no other country to which democratic Greece can turn.

No other nation is willing and able to provide the necessary support for a democratic Greek Government. . . .

The Greek government has been operating in an atmosphere of chaos and extremism. It has made mistakes. The extension of aid by this country does not mean that the United States condones everything that the Greek government has done or will do. We have condemned in the past, and we condemn now, extremist measures of the Right or the Left. We have in the past advised tolerance, and we advise tolerance now.

Greece's neighbor, Turkey, also deserves our attention.

The future of Turkey as an independent and economically sound state is clearly no less important to the freedom-loving people of the world than the future of Greece. The circumstances in which Turkey finds itself today are considerably different from those of Greece. Turkey has been spared the disasters that have beset Greece. And during the war the United States and Great Britain furnished Turkey with material aid. Nevertheless, Turkey now needs our support.

Since the war, Turkey has sought financial assistance from Great Britain and the United States for the purpose of effecting that modernization necessary for the maintenance of its national integrity.

That integrity is essential to the preservation of order in the Middle East.

The British government has informed us that, owing to its own difficulties, it can no longer extend financial or economic aid to Turkey.

As in the case of Greece, if Turkey is to have the assistance it needs, the United States must supply it. We are the only country able to provide that help.

I am fully aware of the broad implications involved if the United States extends assistance to Greece and Turkey, and I shall discuss these implications with you at this time.

One of the primary objectives of the foreign policy of the United States is the creation of conditions in which we and other nations will be able to work out a way of life free from coercion. This was a fundamental issue in the war with Germany and Japan. Our victory was won over countries which sought to impose their will, and their way of life, upon other nations.

To insure the peaceful development of nations, free from coercion, the United States has taken a leading part in establish the United Nations. The United Nations is designed to make possible lasting freedom and independence for all its members. We shall not realize our objectives, however, unless we are willing to help free people to maintain their free institutions and their national integrity against aggressive movements that seek to impose upon them totalitarian regimes. This is no more than a frank recognition that totalitarian regimes imposed on free peoples, by direct or indirect aggression, undermine the foundations of international peace and hence the security of the United States.

The peoples of a number of countries of the world have recently had totalitarian regimes forced upon them against their will. The government of the United States has made frequent protests against coercion and intimidation, in violation of the Yalta agreement, in Poland, Rumania and Bulgaria. I must also state that in a number of other countries there have been similar developments.

At the present moment in world history nearly every nation must choose between alternative ways of life. The choice is too often not a free one.

One way of life is based upon the will of the majority, and is distinguished by free institutions, representative government, free elections, guaranties of individual liberty, freedom of speech and religion and freedom from political oppression.

The second way of life is based upon the will of a minority forcibly imposed upon the majority. It relies upon terror and oppression, a controlled press and radio, fixed elections, and the suppression of personal freedoms.

I believe that it must be the policy of the United States to support peoples who are resisting attempted subjugation by armed minorities or by outside pressures.

I believe that we must assist free peoples to work out their own destinies in their own way.

I believe that our help should be primarily through economic and financial aid which is essential to economic stability and orderly political processes.

The world is not static, and the status quo is not sacred. But we cannot allow changes in the status quo in violation of the charter of the United Nations by such methods as coercion, or by such subterfuges as political infiltration. In helping free and independent nations to maintain their freedom, the United States will be giving effect to the principles of the charter of the United Nations. . . .

The seeds of totalitarian regimes are nurtured by misery and want. They spread and grow in the evil soil of poverty and strife. They reach their full growth when the hope of a people for a better life has died.

We must keep that hope alive.

The free peoples of the world look to us for support in maintaining their freedoms.

If we falter in our leadership, we may endanger the peace of the world-- and we shall surely endanger the welfare of our own nation.

Great responsibilities have been placed upon us by the swift movement of events.

I am confident that the Congress will face these responsibilities squarely.

TRUMAN'S STATEMENT ON KOREA
June 27, 1950

In Korea the Government forces, which were armed to prevent border raids and to preserve internal security, were attacked by invading forces from North Korea. The Security Council of the United Nations called upon the invading troops to cease hostilities and to withdraw to the thirty-eighth parallel. This they have not done, but on the contrary have pressed the attack. The Security Council called upon all members of the United Nations to render every assistance to the United Nations in the execution of this resolution. In these circumstances I have ordered United States air and sea forces to give the Korean Government troops cover and support.

The attack upon Korea makes it plain beyond all doubt that communism has passed beyond the use of subversion to conquer independent nations and will now use armed invasion and war. It has defied the orders of the Security Council of the United Nations issued to preserve international peace and security. In these circumstances the occupation of Formosa by Communist forces would be a direct threat to the security of the Pacific area and to the United States forces performing their lawful and necessary functions in that area.

Accordingly, I have ordered the Seventh Fleet to prevent any attack on Formosa. As a corollary of this action I am calling upon the Chinese Government on Formosa to cease all air and sea operations against the mainland. The Seventh Fleet will see that this is done. The determination of the future status of Formosa must await the restoration of security in the Pacific, a peace settlement with Japan, or consideration by the United Nations.

I have also directed that United States forces in the Philippines be strengthened and that military assistance to the Philippine Government be accelerated.

I have similarly directed acceleration in the furnishing of military assistance to the forces of France and the associated states in Indochina and the consequences of this latest aggression in Korea in defiance of the Charter of the United Nations. A return to the rule of force in international affairs would have far-reaching effects. The United States will continue to uphold the rule of Law.

I have instructed Ambassador Austin, as the representative of the United States to the Security Council, to report these steps to the Council.

THE INTERNAL SECURITY ACT
September 23, 1950

Awaiting and seeking to advance a moment when the United States may be so far extended by foreign engagements, so far divided in counsel, or so far in industrial or financial straits, that overthrow of the Government of the United States by force and violence may seem possible of achievement, it seeks converts far and wide by an extensive system of schooling and indoctrination. Such preparations by Communist organizations in other countries have aided in supplanting existing governments. The Communist organization in the United States, pursuing its stated objectives, the recent control of the world Communist movement itself, present a clear and present danger to the security of the United States and to the existence of free American institutions, and make it necessary that Congress, in order to provide for the common defense, to preserve the sovereignty of the United States as an independent nation, and to guarantee to each State a republican form of government, enact appropriate legislation recognizing the existence of such world-wide conspiracy and designed to prevent it from accomplishing its purpose in the United States....

Sec. 12. (a) There is hereby established a board, to be known as the Subversive Activities Control Board, which shall be composed of five members, who shall be composed of five members, who shall be appointed by the President, by and with the advice and consent of the Senate....

(c) It shall be the duty of the Board--

(1) upon application made by the Attorney General under section 13 (a) of this title, or by any organization under section 13 (b) of this title, to determine whether any organization is a "Communist-action organization" within the meaning of paragraph (3) of section 3 of this title, or a "Communist-front organization" within the meaning of paragraph (4) of section 3 of this title; and ...

Sec. 102. (a) In the event of any one of the following:

(1) Invasion of the territory of the United States or its possessions,

(2) Declaration of war by Congress, or

(3) Insurrection with the United States in aid of a foreign enemy, and if, upon the occurrence of one or more of the above, the President shall find that the proclamation of an emergency pursuant to this section is essential to the preservation, protection and defense of the Constitution, and to the common defense and safety of the territory and people of the Untied States, the

210

President is authorized to make public proclamation of the existence of an "Internal Security Emergency."

(b) A state of "Internal Security Emergency" (hereinafter referred to as the "emergency") so declared shall continue in existence until terminated by proclamation of the President or by concurrent resolution of the Congress....

Sec. 103. (a) Whenever there shall be in existence such an emergency, the President, acting through the Attorney General, is hereby authorized to apprehend and by order detain, pursuant to the provisions of this title, each person as to whom there is reasonable ground to believe that such person probably will engage in, or probably will conspire with others to engage in, acts of espionage or of sabotage....

SENATOR MARGARET CHASE SMITH (R-ME)
SPEAKS OUT AGAINST McCARTHYISM
1950

I think that it is high time for the United States Senate and its Members to do some real soul searching, and to weigh our consciences as to the manner in which we are performing our duty to the people of America, and the manner in which we are using or abusing our individual powers and privileges.

I think it is high time that we remembered that we have sworn to uphold and defend the Constitution. I think it is high time that we remembered that the Constitution, as amended, speaks not only of the freedom of speech but also of trial by accusation.

Whether it be a criminal prosecution in court or a character prosecution in the Senate, there is little practical distinction when the life of a person has been ruined.

Those of us who shout the loudest about Americanism in making character assassinations are all too frequently those who, by our own words and acts, ignore some of the basic principles of Americanism--

The right to criticize.

The right to hold unpopular beliefs.

The right to protest.

The right of independent thought.

The exercise of these rights should not cost one single American citizen his reputation or his right to a livelihood, nor should he be in danger of losing his reputation or livelihood merely because he happens to know someone who holds unpopular beliefs. Who of us does not? Otherwise none of us could call our souls our own. Otherwise thought control would have set in.

The American people are sick and tired of being afraid to speak their minds lest they be politically smeared as Communists or Fascists by their opponents. Freedom of speech is not what it used to be in America. It has been so abused by some that it is not exercised by others.

The American people are sick and tired of seeing innocent people smeared and guilty people whitewashed. But there have been enough proved cases, such as the *Amerasia* case, the Hiss case, the Coplon case, the Gold case, to cause nation-wide distrust and strong suspicion that there may be something to the unproved, sensational accusations. . . .

Today our country is being psychologically divided by the confusion and the suspicions that are bred in the United States Senate to spread like cancerous tentacles of "know nothing, suspect everything" attitudes. . . .

As a United States Senator, I am not proud of the way in which the Senate has been made a publicity platform for irresponsible sensationalism. I am not proud of the reckless abandon in which unproved charges have been hurled from this [Republican] side of the aisle. I am not proud of the obviously staged, undignified countercharges which have been attempted in retaliation from the other [Democratic] side of the aisle.

I do not like the way the Senate has been made a rendezvous for vilification, for selfish political gain at the sacrifice of individual reputations and national unity. I am not proud of the way we smear outsiders from the floor of the Senate and hide behind the cloak of congressional immunity, and still place ourselves beyond criticism on the floor of the Senate.

As an American, I am shocked at the way Republicans and Democrats alike are playing directly into the Communist design of "confuse, divide, and conquer." As an American, I do not want a Democratic administration whitewash or cover-up any more than I want a Republican smear or witch hunt.

As an American, I condemn a Republican Fascist just as much as I condemn a Democratic Communist. I condemn a Democratic Fascist just as much as I condemn a Republican Communist. They are equally dangerous to you and me and to our country. As an American, I want to see our Nation recapture the strength and unity it once had when we fought the enemy instead of ourselves.

BROWN V. BOARD OF EDUCATION,1954

In approaching this problem, we cannot turn the clock back to 1868 when the [14th] Amendment was adopted, or even to 1896 when *Plessy v. Ferguson* was written. We must consider public education in the light of its full development and its present place in American life throughout the Nation. Only in this way can it be determined if segregation in public schools deprives these plaintiffs of the equal protection of the laws.

Today, education is perhaps the most important function of state and local governments. Compulsory school attendance laws and the great expenditures for education both demonstrate our recognition of the importance of education to our democratic society. It is required in the performance of our most basic public responsibilities, even service in the armed forces. It is the very foundation of good citizenship. Today it is a principal instrument in awakening the child to cultural values, in preparing him for later professional training, and in helping him to adjust normally to his environment. In these days, it is doubtful that any child may reasonably be expected to succeed in life if he is denied the opportunity of an education. Such an opportunity, where the state has undertaken to provide it, is a right which must be made available to all on equal terms.

We come then to the question presented: Does segregation of children in public schools solely on the basis of race, even though the physical facilities and other "tangible" factors may be equal, deprive the children of the minority group of equal educational opportunities? We believe that it does....

Such considerations apply with added force to children in grade and high schools. To separate them from others of similar age and qualifications, solely because of their race, generates a feeling of inferiority as to their status in the community that may affect their hearts and minds in a way unlikely ever to be undone. The effect of this separation on their educational opportunities was well stated by a finding in the Kansas case by a court which nevertheless felt compelled to rule against the Negro plaintiffs:

"Segregation of white and colored children in public schools has a detrimental effect upon the colored children. The impact is greater when it has the sanction of the law; for the policy of separating the races is usually interpreted as denoting the inferiority of the Negro group. A sense of inferiority affects the motivation of a child to learn. Segregation with the sanction of law, therefore, has a tendency to [retard] the educational and mental development of Negro children, and to deprive them of some of the benefits they would receive in a racial[ly] integrated school system."

Whatever may have been the extent of psychological knowledge at the time of *Plessy v. Ferguson*, this finding is amply supported by modern authority. Any language in *Plessy v. Ferguson* contrary to this finding is rejected.

We conclude that in the field of public education the doctrine of "separate but equal" has no place. Separate educational facilities are inherently unequal. Therefore, we hold that the plaintiffs and others similarly situated for whom the actions have been brought are, by reason of the segregation complained of, deprived of the equal protection of the laws guaranteed by the Fourteenth Amendment.

Eisenhower Sends Federal Troops, 1957

...I felt that, in speaking from the house of Lincoln, of Jackson, and of Wilson, my words would better convey both the sadness I feel in the action I was compelled today to take and the firmness with which I intend to pursue this course until the orders of the Federal Court at Little Rock can be executed without unlawful interference.

In that city, under the leadership of demagogic extremists, disorderly mobs have deliberately prevented the carrying out of proper orders from a Federal Court. Local authorities have not eliminated that violent opposition and, under the law, I yesterday issued a Proclamation calling upon the mob to disperse.

This morning the mob again gathered in front of the Central High School of Little Rock, obviously for the purpose of again preventing the carrying out of the Court's order relating to the admission of Negro children to that school.

Whenever normal agencies prove inadequate to the task and it becomes necessary for the Executive Branch of the Federal Government to use its powers and authority to uphold Federal Courts, the President's responsibility is inescapable.

In accordance with that responsibility, I have today issued an Executive Order directing the use of troops under Federal authority to aid in the execution of Federal law at Little Rock, Arkansas. This became necessary when my Proclamation of yesterday was not observed, and the obstruction of justice still continues....

Mob rule cannot be allowed to override the decisions of our courts.

Now, let me make it very clear that Federal troops are not being used to relieve local and state authorities of their primary duty to preserve the peace and order of the community...The running of our school system and the maintenance of peace and order in each of our states are strictly local affairs, and the Federal Government does not interfere, except in very special cases and when requested by one of the several states. In the present case the troops are there, pursuant to law, solely for the purpose of preventing interference with the orders of the Court...

At a time when we face grave situations abroad because of the hatred that communism bears toward a system of government based on human rights, it would be difficult to exaggerate the harm that is being done to the prestige and influence and, indeed, to the safety of our nation and the world.

Our enemies are gloating over this incident and using it everywhere to misrepresent our whole nation. We are portrayed as a violator of those standards of conduct which the peoples of the world united to proclaim in the Charter of the United Nations. There they affirmed "faith in fundamental human rights" and "in the dignity and worth of the human person," and they did so "without distinction as to race, sex, language, or religion."

And so, with deep confidence, I call upon citizens of the State of Arkansas to assist in bringing to an immediate end all interference with the law and its processes. If resistance to the Federal Court order ceases at once, the further presence of Federal troops will be unnecessary and the city of Little Rock will return to its normal habits of peace and order--and a blot upon the fair name and high honor of our nation will be removed.

Thus will be restored the image of America and of all its parts as one nation, indivisible, with liberty and justice for all.

DWIGHT D. EISENHOWER'S FAREWELL ADDRESS, 1961

This evening I come to you with a message of leavetaking and farewell, and to share a few final thoughts with you, my countrymen....

We now stand ten years past the midpoint of a century that has witnessed four major wars among great nations--three of these involved our own country. Despite these holocausts America is today the strongest, the most influential and most productive nation in the world. Understandably proud of this pre-eminence, we yet realize that America's leadership and prestige depend, not merely upon our unmatched material progress, riches and military strength, but on how we use our power in the interests of world peace and human betterment.

Throughout American's adventure in free government, our basic purposes have been to keep the peace; to foster progress in human achievement, and to enhance liberty, dignity and integrity among people and among nations. To strive for less would be unworthy of a free and religious people. Any failure traceable to arrogance of our lack of comprehension or readiness to sacrifice would inflict upon us grievous hurt, both a home and abroad.

Progress toward these noble goals is persistently threatened by the conflict now engulfing the world. It commands our whole attention, absorbs our very beings....

Threats, new in kind or degree, constantly arise. Of these, I mention two only.

A vital element in keeping the peace is our military establishment. Our arms must be might, ready for instant action, so that no potential aggressor may be tempted to risk his own destruction.

Our military organization today bears little relation to that known of any of my predecessor in peacetime--or, indeed, by the fighting men of World War II or Korea.

Until the latest of our world conflicts, the United States had no armaments industry. American makers of plowshares could, with time and as required, make swords as well. But we can no longer risk emergency improvisation of national defense. We have been compelled to create a permanent armaments industry of vast proportions. added to this, three and a half million men and women are directly engaged in the defense establishment. We annually spend on military security alone more than the net income of all United States corporations.

Now this conjunction of an immense military establishment and a large arms industry is new in the American experience. The total influence--economic, political, even spiritual--is felt in every city, every state house, every office of the Federal Government. We recognize the imperative need for this development. Yet we must not fail to comprehend its grave implications. Our toil, resources and livelihood are all involved; so is the very structure of our society.

In the councils of Government, we must guard against the acquisition of unwarranted influence, whether sought or unsought, by the military-industrial complex. The potential for the disastrous rise of misplaced power exists and will persist.

We must never let the weight of this combination endanger our liberties or democratic processes. We should take nothing for granted. Only an alert and knowledgeable citizenry can compel the proper meshing of the huge industrial and military machinery of defense with our peaceful methods and goals, so that security and liberty may prosper together.

JOHN F. KENNEDY'S INAUGURAL ADDRESS, 1961

We observe today not a victory of party but a celebration of freedom--symbolizing an end as well as a beginning--signifying renewal as well as change. For I have sworn before you and Almighty God the same solemn oath our forebears prescribed nearly a century and three-quarters ago.

The world is very different now. For man holds in his mortal hands the power to abolish all forms of human poverty and all forms of human life. And yet the same revolutionary beliefs for which our forebears fought are still at issue around the globe--the belief that the rights of man come not from the generosity of the state but from the hand of God.

We dare not forget today that we are the heirs of that first revolution. Let the word go forth from this time and place, to friend and foe alike, that the torch has been passed to a new generation of Americans--born in this century, tempered by war, disciplined by a hard and bitter peace, proud of our ancient heritage--and unwilling to witness or permit the slow undoing of those human rights to which this nation has always been committed, and to which we are committed today at home and around the world.

Let every nation know, whether it wishes use well or ill, that we shall pay any price, bear any burden, meet any hardship, support any friend, oppose any foe to assure the survival and the success of liberty.

To our sister republics south of our border, we offer a special pledge--to convert our good words into good deeds--in a new alliance for progress--to assist free men and free governments in casting off the chains of poverty. But this peaceful revolution of hope cannot become the prey of hostile powers. Let all our neighbors know that we shall join with them to oppose aggression or subversion anywhere in the Americas. And let every other power know that this hemisphere intends to remain the master of its own house.

Finally, to those nations who would make themselves our adversary, we offer not a pledge but a request: that both sides begin anew the quest for peace, before the dark powers of destruction unleashed by science engulf all humanity in planned or accidental self-destruction.

But neither can two great and powerful groups of nations take comfort from our present course-both sides overburdened by the coast of modern weapons, both rightly alarmed by the steady spread of the deadly atom, yet both racing to alter that uncertain balance of terror that stays the hand of mankind's final war.

So let us begin anew--remembering on both sides that civility is not a sign of weakness, and sincerity is always subject to proof. Let us never negotiate out of fear. But let us never fear to negotiate.

Let both sides explore what problems unite us instead of belaboring those problems which divide us.

Let both sides, for the first time, formulate serious and precise proposals for the inspection and control of arms--and bring the absolute power to destroy other nations under the absolute control of all nations.

All this will note be finished in the first 100 days. Nor will it be finished in the first 1,000 days, nor in the life of this Administration, nor even perhaps in our lifetime on this planet. But let us begin.

In your hands, my fellow citizens, more than mine, will rest the final success or failure of our course. Since this country was founded, each generation of Americans has been summoned to give testimony to its national loyalty. The graves of young Americans who answered the call to service surround the globe.

Now the trumpet summons us again--not as a call to bear arms, though arms we need--not as a call to battle, though embattled we are--but a call to bear the burden of a long twilight struggle year in and year out, "rejoicing in hope, patient in tribulation"--a struggle against the common enemies of man: tyranny, poverty, disease and war itself.

And so, my fellow Americans: ask not what your country can do for you-- ask what you can do for your country.

My fellow citizens of the world: ask not what American will do for you, but what together we can do for the freedom of man.

JOHN F. KENNEDY ON THE CUBAN MISSILE CRISIS, 1962

This government, as promised, has maintained the closest surveillance of the Soviet military build-up on the island of Cuba. Within the past week, unmistakable evidence has established the fact that a series of offensive missile sites is now in preparation on that imprisoned island. The purpose of these bases can be none other than to provide a nuclear strike capability against the Western Hemisphere...

For many years, both the Soviet Union and the United States...have deployed strategic nuclear weapons with great care, never upsetting the precarious status quo which insured that these weapons would not be used in the absence of some vital challenge. Our own strategic missiles have never been transferred to the territory of any other nation under a cloak of secrecy and deception; and our history--unlike that of the Soviets since the end of World War II--demonstrates that we have no desire to dominate or conquer any other nation or impose our system upon its people. Nevertheless, American citizens have become adjusted to living daily on the bull's-eye of Soviet missiles located inside the U.S.S.R. or in submarines.

In that sense, missiles in Cuba, add to an already clear and present danger...

But this secret, swift, and extraordinary buildup of Communist missiles-- in an area well known to have a special and historical relationship to the United States and the nations of the Western Hemisphere, in violation of Soviet assurances, and in defiance of American and hemispheric policy--this sudden, clandestine decision to station strategic weapons for the first time outside of Soviet soil--is a deliberately provocative and unjustified change in the status quo which cannot be accepted by this country, if our courage and our commitments are ever to be trusted again by either friend or foe...

Our policy has been one of patience and restraint, as befits a peaceful and powerful nation, which leads a worldwide alliance...We will not prematurely or unnecessarily risk the costs of worldwide nuclear war in which even the fruits of victory would be ashes in our mouth--but neither will we shrink from that risk at any time it must be faced...

The path we have chosen for the present is full of hazards, as all paths are--but it is the one most consistent with our character and our courage as a nation and our commitments around the world. The cost of freedom is always high--but Americans have always paid it. And one path we shall never choose, and that is the path of surrender or submission.

Acting, therefore, in the defense of our own security and of the entire Western Hemisphere,...I have directed that the following *initial* steps be taken immediately:

First: To halt this offensive buildup, a strict quarantine on all offensive military equipment under shipment to Cuba is being initiated. All ships of any kind bound for Cuba from whatever nation or port will, if found to contain cargoes of offensive weapons, be turned back. This quarantine will be extended, if needed, to other types of cargo and carriers. we are not at this time, however, denying the necessities of life, as the Soviets attempted to do in their Berlin blockade of 1948.

Second: I have directed the continued and increased close [aerial] surveillance of Cuba and its military buildup...

Third: It shall be the policy of this Nation to regard any nuclear missile launched from Cuba against any nation in the Western Hemisphere as an attack by the Soviet Union on the United States, requiring a full retaliatory response upon the Soviet Union.

Fourth: As a necessary military precaution, I have reinforced our base at Guantanamo [Cuba], evacuated today the dependents of our personnel there, and ordered additional military units to be on a standby alert basis.

Fifth: We are calling tonight for an immediate meeting of the Organ of Consultation under the Organization of American States, to consider this threat to hemispheric security and to invoke Articles 6 and 8 of the Rio Treaty in support of all necessary action...Our other allies around the world have also been alerted.

Sixth: Under the Charter of the United Nations, we are asking tonight that an emergency meeting of the Security Council be convoked without delay to take action against this latest Soviet threat to world peace. Our resolution will call for the prompt dismantling and withdrawal of all offensive weapons in Cuba, under the supervision of U.N. observers, before the quarantine can be lifted.

Seventh and finally: I call upon Chairman Khrushchev to halt and eliminate this clandestine, reckless, and provocative threat to world peace and to stable relations between our two nations. I call upon him further to abandon this course of world domination, and to join in an historic effort to end the perilous arms race and to transform the history of man.

JOHN F. KENNEDY ON THE "STRATEGY OF PEACE", 1963

But I also believe that we must reexamine our own attitudes--as individuals and as a nation--for our attitude is as essential as theirs. And every graduate of this school, every thoughtful citizen who despairs of war and wishes to bring peace, should begin by looking inward--by examining his own attitude towards the course of the cold war and toward freedom and peace here at home.

First: Examine our attitude towards peace itself. Too many of us think it is impossible. Too many think it is unreal. But that is a dangerous, defeatist belief. It leads to the conclusion that war is inevitable--that mankind is doomed--that we are gripped by forces we cannot control.

We need not accept that view. Our problems are man-made. Therefore, they can be solved by man. And man can be as big as he wants. No problem of human destiny is beyond human beings. Man's reason and spirit have often solved the seemingly unsolvable--and we believe they can do it again.

I am not referring to the absolute, infinite concepts of universal peace and goodwill of which some fantasies and fanatics dream. I do not deny the value of hopes and dreams but we merely invite discouragement and incredulity by making that our only and immediate goal.

Let us focus instead on a more practical, more attainable peace--based not on a sudden revolution in human nature but on a gradual evolution in human institutions--on a series of concrete actions and effective agreements which are in the interests of all concerned.

There is no single, simple key to this peace--no grand or magic formula to be adopted by one or two powers. genuine peace must be the product of many nations, the sum of many acts. It must be dynamic, not static, changing to meet the challenge of each new generation. For peace is a process--a way of solving problems.

With such a peace, there will still be quarrels and conflicting interests, as there are within families and nations. World peace, like community peace, does not require that each man love his neighbor--it requires only that they live together with mutual tolerance, submitting their disputes to a just and peaceful settlement. And history teaches us that enmities between nations, as between individuals, do not last forever. However fixed our likes and dislikes may seem the tide of time and events will often bring surprising changes in the relations between nations and neighbors.

So let us persevere. Peace need not be impracticable--and war need not be inevitable. By defining our goal more clearly--by making it seem more manageable and less remote--we can help all people to see it, to draw hope from it, and to move irresistibly towards it.

And second: Let us re-examine our attitude towards the Soviet Union. It is discouraging to think that their leaders may actually believe what their propagandists write.

It is discouraging to read a recent authoritative Soviet text on military strategy and find, on page after page, wholly baseless and incredible claims-- such as the allegation that "American imperialist circles are preparing to unleash different types of war...that there is a very real threat of a preventative war being unleashed by American imperialists against the Soviet Union...(and that) the political aims," and I quote, "of the American imperialists are to enslave economically and politically the European and other capitalist countries...(and) to achieve world domination...by means of aggressive war."

Truly, as it was written long ago: "The wicked flee when no man pursueth." Yet it is sad to read these Soviet statements--to realize the extent of the gulf between us. But it is also a warning--a warning to the American people not to fall into the same trap as the soviets, not to see only a distorted and desperate view of the other side, not to see conflict as inevitable, accommodation as impossible and communication as nothing more than an exchange of threats.

No government or social system is so evil that its people must be considered as lacking in virtue. As Americans, we find Communism profoundly repugnant as a negation of personal freedom and dignity. But we can still hail the Russian people for their many achievements--in science and space, in economic and industrial growth, in culture, in acts of courage.

Among the many traits the peoples of our two countries have in common, none is stronger than our mutual abhorrence of war. Almost unique among the major world powers, we have never been at war with each other. And no nation in the history of battle ever suffered more than the Soviet Union in the second world war. At least 20,000,000 lost their lives, Countless millions of homes and families were burned or sacked. A third of the nation's territory, including two-thirds of its industrial base, was turned into a wasteland--a loss equivalent to the destruction of this country east of Chicago.

Today, should total war ever break out again--no matter how--our two countries will be the primary targets. It is an ironic but accurate fact that the two strongest powers are the two in the most danger of devastation. All we have built, all we have worked for, would be destroyed in the first 24 hours. And even in the cold war--which brings burdens and dangers to so many countries, including this nation's closest allies--our two countries bear the

224

heaviest burdens. For we are both devoting massive sums of money to weapons that could be better devoted to combat ignorance, poverty and disease.

We are both caught up in a vicious and dangerous cycle and suspicion on one side breeding suspicion on the other, and new weapons begetting counter-weapons.

In short, both the United States and its allies, and the Soviet Union and its allies, have a mutually deep interest in a just and genuine peace and in halting the arms race. Agreements to this end are in the interests of the Soviet Union as well as ours--and even the most hostile nations can be relied upon to accept and keep those treaty obligations and only those treaty obligations, which are in their own interest.

So, let us not be blind to our differences--but let us also direct attention to our common interests and the means by which those differences can be resolved. And if we cannot end now our differences, at least we can help make the world safe for diversity. For, in the final analysis, our most basic common link is that we all inhabit this small planet. We all breathe the same air. We all cherish our children's future. And we are all mortal.

Third: Let us re-examine our attitude towards the cold war, remembering we are not engaged in a debate, seeking to pile up debating points. We are not here distributing blame or pointing the finger of judgment. We must deal with the world as it is, and not as it might have been had the history of the last eighteen years been different.

We must, therefore, persevere in the search for peace in the hope that constructive changes within the Communist bloc might bring within reach solutions which now seem beyond us. We must conduct our affairs in such a way that it becomes in the Communists' interest to agree on a genuine peace. And above all, while defending our own vital interests, nuclear powers must avert those confrontations which bring an adversary to a choice of either a humiliating retreat or a nuclear war. To adopt that kind of course in the nuclear age would be evidence only of the bankruptcy of our policy--or of a collective death-wish for the world.

To secure these ends, America's weapons are non-provocative, carefully controlled, designed to deter and capable of selective use. Our military forces are committed to peace and disciplined in self-restraint. Our diplomats are instructed to avoid unnecessary irritants and purely rhetorical hostility.

For we can seek a relaxation of tensions without relaxing our guard. And, for our part, we do not need to use threats to prove that we are resolute. We do not need to jam foreign broadcasts out of fear our faith will be eroded.

We are unwilling to impose our system on any unwilling people--but we are willing and able to engage in peaceful competition with any people on earth.

Meanwhile, we seek to strengthen the United Nations, to help solve its financial problems, to make it a more effective instrument for peace, to develop it into a genuine world security system--a system capable of resolving disputes on the basis of law, of insuring the security of the large and the small, and of creating conditions under which arms can finally be abolished.

At the same time we seek to keep peace inside the non-Communist world, where many nations, all of them our friends, are divided over issues which weaken Western unity, which invite Communist intervention, or which threaten to erupt into war.

Our efforts in West New Guinea, in the Congo, in the Middle East and the Indian subcontinent have been persistent and patient despite criticism from both sides. We have tried to set an example for others--by seeking to adjust small but significant differences with our own closest neighbors in Mexico and Canada.

Speaking of other nations, I wish to make one point clear. We are bound to many nations by alliances. These alliances exist because our concern and theirs substantially overlap. Our commitment to defend Western Europe and West Berlin, for example, stand undiminished because of the identity of our vital interests. The United States will make no deal with the Soviet Union at the expense of other nations and other peoples, not merely because they are our partners, but also because their interests and ours converge.

Our interests converge, however, not only in defending the frontiers of freedom, but in pursuing the paths of peace.

It is our hope--and the purpose of allied policies--to convince the Soviet Union that she, too, should let each nation choose its own future, so long as that choice does not interfere with the choices of others. The communist drive to impose their political and economic system on others is the primary cause of world tension today. For there can be no doubt that, if all nations could refrain from interfering in the self-determination of others, the peace would be much more assured.

This will require a new effort to achieve world law--a new context for world discussions. It will require increased understanding between the Soviets and ourselves. And increased understanding will require increased contact and communication.

One step in this direction is the proposed arrangement for a direct line between Moscow and Washington, to avoid on each side the dangerous delays, misunderstanding, and misreadings of the other's actions which might occur in a time of crisis.

We have also been talking in Geneva about other first-step measures of arms control, designed to limit the intensity of the arms race and reduce the risks of accidental war.

Our primary long-range interest in Geneva, however, is general and complete disarmament--designed to take place by stages, permitting parallel political developments to build the new institutions of peace which would take the place of arms. The pursuit of disarmament has been an effort of this Government since the 1920's. It has been urgently sought by the past three Administrations. And however dim the prospects are today, we intend to continue this effort--to continue it in order that all countries, including our own, can better grasp what the problems and the possibilities of disarmament are.

The only major area of these negotiations where the end is in sight--yet where a fresh start is badly needed--is in a treaty to outlaw nuclear tests. The conclusion of such a treaty--so near and yet so far--would check the spiraling arms race in one of its most dangerous areas. It would place the nuclear powers in a position to deal more effectively with one of the greatest hazards which man faces in 1963--the further spread of nuclear weapons. It would increase our security--it would decrease the prospects of war.

Surely this goal is sufficiently important to require our steady pursuit, yielding neither to the temptation to give up the whole effort nor the temptation to give up our insistence on vital and responsible safeguards.

I am taking this opportunity, therefore, to announce two important decisions in this regard:

First: Chairman Khrushchev, Prime Minister Macmillan and I have agreed that high-level discussions will shortly begin in Moscow towards early agreement on a comprehensive test ban treaty. Our hopes must be tempered with the caution of history--but with our hopes go the hopes of all mankind.

Second: To make clear our good faith and solemn convictions on the matter, I now declare that the United States does not propose to conduct nuclear tests in the atmosphere so long as other states do not do so. We will not be the first to resume. Such a declaration is no substitute for a formal binding treaty--but I hope it will help us achieve one. Nor would such a treaty be a substitute for disarmament--but I hope it will help us achieve it.

Finally, my fellow Americans, let us examine our attitude towards peace and freedom here at home. The quality and spirit of our own society must justify and support our efforts abroad. We must show it in the dedication of our own lives--as many of you who are graduating today will have an

227

opportunity to do, by serving without pay in the Peace Corps abroad or in the proposed National Service Corps here at home.

But wherever we are, we must all, in our daily lives, live up to the age-old faith that peace and freedom walk together. In too many of our cities today, the peace is not secure because freedom is incomplete.

It is the responsibility of the executive branch at all levels of government--local, state and national-- to provide and protect that freedom for all of our citizens by all means within our authority. It is the responsibility of the legislative branch at all levels, wherever the authority is not now adequate, to make it adequate. And it is the responsibility of all citizens in all sections of this country to respect the rights of others and respect the law of the land.

All this is not unrelated to world peace. "When a man's ways please the Lord," the scriptures tell us, "he maketh even his enemies to be at peace with him." And is not peace, in the last analysis, basically a matter of human rights--the right to live out our lives without fear of devastation--the right to breathe air as nature provided it--the right of future generations to a healthy existence?

While we proceed to safeguard our national interests, let us also safeguard human interests. And the elimination of war and arms is clearly in the interest of both.

No treaty, however much it may be to the advantage of all, however tightly it may be worded, can provide absolute security against the risks of deception and evasion. But it can--if it is sufficiently effective in its interests of its signers--offer far more security and far fewer risks than an unabated, uncontrolled, unpredictable arms race.

The United States, as the world knows, will never start a war. We do not want a war. We do not now expect a war. This generation of Americans has already had enough--more than enough--of war and hate and oppression. We shall be prepared if others wish it. We shall be alert to try to stop it. But we shall also do our part to build a world of peace where the weak are safe and the strong are just.

We are not helpless before that task or hopeless of its success. Confident and unafraid, we labor on--not toward a strategy of annihilation but toward a strategy of peace. Thank you.

GULF OF TONKIN RESOLUTION, 1964

Whereas naval units of the Communist regime in Vietnam, in violation of the principles of the Charter of the United Nations and of international law, have deliberately and repeatedly attacked the United States naval vessels present in international waters, and have thereby created a serious threat to international peace;

Whereas these attacks are part of a deliberate and systematic campaign of aggression that the Communist regime in North Vietnam has been waging against its neighbors and the nations joined with them in the collective defense of their freedom;

Whereas the United States is assisting the peoples *of southeast Asia to protect their political freedom and has not territorial, military or political ambitions in that area, but desires only that these peoples should be left in peace to work out their own destinies in their own way: Now, therefore, be it*

Resolved by the Senate and House of Representatives of the United States of America in Congress assembled, That the Congress approves and supports the determination of the President, as Commander in Chief, to take all necessary measures to repel any armed attack against the forces of the United States and to prevent further aggression.

Sec. 2. The United States regards as vital to its national interests and to world peace the maintenance of international peace and security in southeast Asia.... The United States is, therefore, prepared, as the President determines, to take all necessary steps, including the use of armed force, to assist any member or protocol state of the Southeast Asia Collective Defense Treaty requesting assistance in defense of its freedom.

Sec. 3. This resolution shall expire when the President shall determine that the peace and security of the area is reasonably assured....

LYNDON B. JOHNSON AND THE "GREAT SOCIETY," 1964

I have called for a national war on poverty. Our objective: total victory.

There are millions of Americans--one fifth of our people--who have not shared in the abundance which has been granted to most of us, and on whom the gates of opportunity have been closed.

What does this poverty mean to those who endure it?

It means a daily struggle to secure the necessities for even a meager existence. It means that the abundance, the comforts, the opportunities they see all around them are beyond their grasp.

Worst of all, it means hopelessness for the young.

The young Man or woman who grows up without a decent education, in a broken home, in a hostile and squalid environment, in ill health or in the face of racial injustice--that young man or woman is often trapped in a life of poverty.

He does not have the skills demanded by a complex society. He does not know how to acquire those skills. He faces a mounting sense of despair which drains initiative and ambition and energy...

The war on poverty is not a struggle simply to support people, to make them dependent on the generosity of others.

It is a struggle to give people a chance.

It is an effort to allow them to develop and use their capacities, as we have been allowed to develop and use ours, so that they can share, as others share, in the promise of this nation.

We do this, first of all, because it is right that we should.

From the establishment of public education and land grant colleges through agricultural extension and encouragement to industry, we have pursued the goal of a nation with full and increasing opportunities for all its citizens.

The war on poverty is a further step in that pursuit.

We do it also because helping some will increase the prosperity of all.

Our fight against poverty will be an investment in the most valuable of our resources--the skills and strength of our people.

And in the future, as in the past, this investment will return its cost many fold to our entire economy.

If we can raise the annual earnings of 10 million among the poor by only $1,000 we will have added 14 billion dollars a year to our national output. In addition we can make important reductions in public assistance payments which now cost us 4 billion dollars a year, and in the large costs of fighting crime and delinquency, disease and hunger.

This is only part of the story.

Our history has proved that each time we broaden the base of abundance, giving more people the chance to produce and consume, we create new industry, higher production, increased earnings and better income for all.

Giving new opportunity to those who have little will enrich the lives of all the rest.

Because it is right, because it is wise, and because, for the first time in our history, it is possible to conquer poverty, I submit, for the consideration of the Congress and the country, the Economic Opportunity Act of 1964.

The Act does not merely expand old programs or improve what is already being done.

It charts a new course.

It strikes at the causes, not just the consequences of poverty.

It can be a milestone in our one-hundred-eighty year search for a better life for our people.

PRESIDENT JOHNSON SUPPORTS CIVIL RIGHTS, 1965

Mr. Speaker, Mr. President, Members of the Congress:

I speak tonight for the dignity of man and the destiny of democracy.

I urge every member of both parties, Americans of all religions and of all colors, from every section of this country, to join me in that cause.

Our mission is at once the oldest and the most basic of this country: to right wrong, to do justice, to serve man.

In our time we have come to live with moments of great crisis. Our lives have been marked with debate about great issues; issues of war and peace, issues of prosperity and depression. But rarely in any time does an issue lay bare the secret heart of America itself. Rarely are we met with a challenge, not to our growth or abundance, our welfare or our security, but rather to the values and the purposes and the meaning of our beloved Nation.

The issue of equal rights for American Negroes is such an issue. And should we defeat every enemy, should we double our wealth and conquer the stars, and still be unequal to this issue, then we will have failed as a people and as a nation.

For with a country as with a person, "What is a man profited, if he shall gain the whole world, and lose his own soul?"

There is no Negro problem. There is no Southern problem. There is no Northern problem. There is only an American problem. And we are met here tonight as Americans--not as Democrats or Republicans--we are met here as Americans to solve that problem.

This was the first nation in the history of the world to be founded with a purpose. The great phrases of that purpose still sound in every American heart, North and South: All men are created equal"--"government by consent of the governed"--"give me liberty or give me death." Well, those are not just clever words, or those are not just empty theories. In their name Americans have fought and died for two centuries, and tonight around the world they stand there as guardians of our liberty, risking their lives.

Those words are a promise to every citizen that he shall share in the dignity of man. This dignity cannot be found in a man's possessions; it cannot be found in his power, or in his position. It really rests on his right to be treated as a man equal in opportunity to all others. It says that he shall share in freedom, he shall choose his leaders, educate his children, and provide for his family according to his ability and his merits as a human being.

232

To apply any other test--to deny a man his hopes because of his color or race, his religion or the place of his birth--is not only to do injustice, it is to deny America and to dishonor the dead who gave their lives for American freedom.

....I will send to Congress a law designed to eliminate illegal barriers to the right to vote....

This bill will strike down restrictions to voting in all elections--Federal, State, and local--which have been used to deny Negroes the right to vote.

This bill will establish a simple, uniform standard which cannot be used, however ingenious the effort, to flout our Constitution.

It will provide for citizens to be registered by officials of the United States Government if the State officials refuse to register them....

There is no constitutional issue here. The command of the Constitution is plain.

There is no moral issue. It is wrong--deadly wrong--to deny any of your fellow Americans the right to vote in this country.

There is no issue of States rights or national rights. There is only the struggle for human rights.

I have not the slightest doubt what will be your answer....

This time, on this issue, there must be no delay, no hesitation and no compromise with our purpose.

We cannot, we must not, refuse to protect the right of every American to vote in every election that he may desire to participate in. And we ought not and we cannot and we must not wait another 8 months before we get a bill. We have already waited a hundred years and more, and the time for waiting is gone....

But even if we pass this bill, the battle will not be over. What happened in Selma is part of a far larger movement which reaches into every section and State of America. It is the effort of American Negroes to secure for themselves the full blessings of American life.

PRESIDENT JOHNSON ASSERTS HIS WAR AIMS, 1965

...Why are we in South Viet-Nam?

We are there because we have a promise to keep. Since 1954 every American President has offered support to the people of South Viet-Nam. We have helped to build, and we have helped to defend. Thus, over many years, we have made a national pledge to help South Viet-Nam defend its independence.

And I intend to keep that promise.

To dishonor that pledge, to abandon this small and brave nation to its enemies, and to the terror that must follow, would be an unforgivable wrong.

We are also there to strengthen world order. Around the globe from Berlin to Thailand are people whose well being rests in part on the belief that they can count on us [to honor some forty defensive alliances] if they are attacked. To leave Viet-Nam to its fate would shake the confidence of all these people in the value of an American commitment and in the value of America's word. The result would be increased unrest and instability, and even wider war.

We are also there because there are great stakes in the balance. Let no one think for a moment that retreat from Viet-Nam would bring an end to conflict. The battle would be renewed in one country and then another. The central lesson of our time is that the appetite of aggression is never satisfied....

Our objective is the independence of South Viet-Nam and its freedom from attack. We want nothing for ourselves--only that the people of South Viet-Nam be allowed to guide their own country in their own way.

We will do everything necessary to reach that objective and we will do only what is absolutely necessary.

THE KERNER REPORT, 1967

On July 28, 1967, the President of the United States established this Commission and directed us to answer three basic questions:

What happened?

Why did it happen?

What can be done to prevent it from happening again?

To respond to these questions, we have undertaken a broad range of studies and investigations. We have visited the riot cities; we have heard many witnesses; we have sought the counsel of experts across the country.

This is our basic conclusion: Our nation is moving toward two societies, one black, one white--separate and unequal.

Reaction to last summer's disorders has quickened the movement and deepened the division. Discrimination and segregation have long permeated much of American life; they now threaten the future of every American.

This deepening racial division is not inevitable. The movement apart can be reversed. Choice is still possible. Our principal task is to define that choice and to press for a national resolution.

To pursue our present course will involve the continuing polarization of the American community and, ultimately, the destruction of basic democratic values.

The alternative is not blind repression or capitulation to lawlessness. It is the realization of common opportunities for all within a single society.

This alternative will require a commitment to national action--compassionate, massive and sustained, backed by the resources of the most powerful and the richest nation on this earth. From every American it will require new attitudes, new understanding, and, above all, new will.

The vital needs of the nation must be met; hard choices must be made, and, if necessary, new taxes enacted.

Violence cannot build a better society. Disruption and disorder nourish repression, not justice. They strike at the freedom of every citizen. The community cannot--it will not-- tolerate coercion and mob rule.

Violence and destruction must be ended--in the streets of the ghetto and in the lives of people.

Segregation and poverty have created in the racial ghetto a destructive environment totally unknown to most white Americans.

What white Americans have never fully understood--but what the Negro can never forget--is that white society is deeply implicated in the ghetto. White institutions created it, white institutions maintain it, and white society condones it.

It is time now to turn with all the purpose at our command to the major unfinished business of this nation. It is time to adopt strategies for action that will produce quick and visible progress. It is time to make good the promises of American democracy to all citizens--urban and rural, white and black, Spanish-surname, American Indian, and every minority group.

Our recommendations embrace three basic principles:

- To mount programs on a scale equal to the dimension of the problems;

- To aim these programs for high impact in the immediate future in order to close the gap between promise and performance;

- To undertake new initiatives and experiments that can change the system of failure and frustration that now dominates the ghetto and weakens our society.

RICHARD NIXON ON SENDING U.S. TROOPS TO CAMBODIA
1970

Ten days ago, in my report to the Nation on Viet-Nam, I announced a decision to withdraw an additional 150,000 Americans from Viet-Nam over the next year. I said then that I was making that decision despite our concern over increased enemy activity in Laos, in Cambodia, and in South Viet-Nam.

After full consultation with the national Security Council...and my other advisers, I have concluded that the actions of the enemy in the last 10 days clearly endanger the lives of Americans who are in Viet-Nam now and would constitute an unacceptable risk to those who will be there after withdrawal of another 150,000.

To protect our men who are in Viet-Nam and to guarantee the continued success of our withdrawal and Vietnamization programs, I have concluded that the time has come for action....

For the past 5 years...North Viet-Nam has occupied military sanctuaries all along the Cambodian frontier with South Viet-Nam. Some of these extend up to 20 miles into Cambodia. The sanctuaries...are on both sides of the border. They are used for hit-and-run attacks on American and South Vietnamese forces in South Viet-Nam.

These Communist-occupied territories contain major base camps, training sites, logistics facilities, weapons and ammunition factories, airstrips, and prisoner of war compounds....

Tonight American and South Vietnamese units will attack the headquarters for the entire Communist military operation in South Viet-Nam. This key control center has been occupied by the North Vietnamese and Viet Cong for 5 years in blatant violation of Cambodia's neutrality.

This is not an invasion of Cambodia. the areas in which these attacks will be launched are completely occupied and controlled by North Vietnamese forces. Our purpose is not to occupy the areas. Once enemy forces are driven out of these sanctuaries and once their military supplies are destroyed, we will withdraw.

Now, let me give you the reasons for my decision.

A majority of the American people, a majority of you listening to me, are for the withdrawal of our forces from Viet-Nam. The action I have taken tonight is indispensable for the continuing success of that withdrawal program.

A majority of the American people want to end this war rather than to have it drag on interminably. The action I have taken tonight will serve that purpose.

A majority of the American people want to keep the casualties of our brave men in Viet-Nam at an absolute minimum. The action I have taken tonight is essential if we are to accomplish that goal.

We take this action not for the purpose of expanding the war into Cambodia, but for the purpose of ending the war in Viet-Nam and winning the just peace we all desire. We have made and we will continue to make every possible effort to end this war through negotiation at the conference table rather than through more fighting on the battlefield....

My fellow Americans, we live in an age of anarchy, both abroad and at home. We see mindless attacks on all the great institutions which have been created by free civilizations in the last 500 years. Even here in the United States, great universities are being systematically destroyed. Small nations all over the world find themselves under attack from within and from without.

If, when the chips are down, the world's most powerful nation, the United States of America, acts like a pitiful, helpless giant, the forces of totalitarianism and anarchy will threaten free nations and free institutions throughout the world.

It is not our power but our will and character that is being tested tonight. The question all Americans must ask and answer tonight is this: Does the richest and strongest nation in the history of the world have the character to meet a direct challenge by a group which rejects every effort to win a just peace, ignores our warning, tramples on solemn agreements, violates the neutrality of an unarmed people, and uses our prisoners as hostages?

I promised to end this war. I shall keep that promise.

I promised to win a just peace. I shall keep that promise.

WHITE HOUSE CONVERSATIONS
June 23, 1972

HALDEMAN: Now, on the investigation, you know the Democratic break-in thing, we're back in the problem area because the FBI is not under control, because [Director Patrick] Gray doesn't exactly know how to control it and they have--their investigation is now leading into some productive areas. ...They've been able to trace the money--not through the money itself--but through the bank sources--the banker. And it goes in some directions we don't want it to go. Ah, also there have been some [other] things--like an informant came in off the street to the FBI in Miami who was a photographer or has a friend who is a photographer who developed some films through this buy [Bernard] Barker and the films had pictures of Democratic National Committee letterhead documents and things. So it's things like that are filtering in. ...[John] Mitchell came up with yesterday, and John Dean analyzed very carefully last night and concludes, concurs now with Mitchell's recommendation that the only way to solve this...is for us to have [CIA Assistant Director Vernon] Walters call Pat Gray and just say, "Stay to hell out of this--this is ah, [our] business here. We don't want you to go any further on it." That's not an unusual development and ah, that would take care of it.

PRESIDENT: What about Pat Gray--you mean Pat Gray doesn't want to?

HALDEMAN: Pat does want to. He doesn't know how to, and he doesn't have any basis for doing it. Given this, he will then have the basis. He'll call [FBI Assistant Director] Mark Felt in, and the two of them--and Mark Felt wants to cooperate because he's ambitious--

PRESIDENT: Yeah.

HALDEMAN: He'll call him in and say, "We've got the signal from across the river to put the hold on this." And that will fit rather well because the FBI agents who are working the case, at this point feel that's what it is.

PRESIDENT: This is CIA? They've traced the money? Who'd they trace it to?...

HALDEMAN: Ken Dahlberg.

PRESIDENT: Who the hell is Ken Dahlberg?

HALDEMAN: He gave $25,000 in Minnesota and, ah, the check went directly to this guy Barker.

PRESIDENT: It isn't from the Committee though, from [Maurice] Stans?

HALDEMAN: Yeah. It is. It's directly traceable and there's some more through some Texas people that went to the Mexican bank which can also be traced to the Mexican bank--they'll get their names today.

PRESIDENT: Well, I mean, there's no way--I'm just thinking if they don't cooperate, what do they say? That they were approached by the Cubans? That's what Dahlberg has to say, the Texans too.

HALDEMAN: Well, if they will. But then we're relying on more and more people all the time. That's the problem and they'll [the FBI]...stop if we could take this other route.

PRESIDENT: All right.

HALDEMAN: [Mitchell and Dean] say they only way to do that is from White House Instructions. And it's got to be to [CIA director Richard] Helms and to--ah, what's his name?...Walters....And the proposal would be that...[John] Ehrlichman and I call them in, and say, ah--

PRESIDENT: All right, fine. How do you call him in--I mean you just-- well, we protected Helms from one hell of a lot of things.

HALDEMAN: That's what Ehrlichman says.

PRESIDENT: Of course; this [Howard] Hunt [business.] That will uncover a lot of things. You open that scab there's a hell of a lot of things and we just feel that it would be very detrimental to have this thing go any further. This involves these Cubans, Hunt, and a lot of hanky-panky that we have nothing to do with ourselves. Well, what the hell, did Mitchell know about this?

HALDEMAN: I think so. I don't think he knew the details, but I think he knew.

PRESIDENT: He didn't know how it was going to be handled though-- with Dahlberg and the Texans and so forth? Well who was the asshole that did? Is it [G. Gordon] Liddy? Is that the fellow? He must be a little nuts!

HALDEMAN: He is.

PRESIDENT: I mean he just isn't well screwed on, is he? Is that the problem?

HALDEMAN: No, but he was under pressure, apparently, to get more information, and as he got more pressure, he pushed the people harder.

PRESIDENT: Pressure from Mitchell?

HALDEMAN: Apparently....

PRESIDENT: All right, fine, I understand it all. We won't second-guess Mitchell and the rest. Thank God it wasn't [special White House counsel Charles] Colson.

HALDEMAN: The FBI interviewed Colson yesterday. They determined that would be a good thing to do. To have him take an interrogation, which he did, and the FBI guys working the case concluded that there were one or two possibilities--one, that this was a White House (they don't think that there is anything at the Election Committee) they think it was either a White House operation and they had some obscure reasons for it--non-political, or it was a--Cuban [operation] and [involved] the CIA. And after the interrogation of Colson yesterday, they concluded it was not the White House, but are now convinced it is a CIA thing, so the CIA turnoff would--

PRESIDENT: Well, not sure of their analysis, I'm not going to get that involved. I'm (unintelligible).

HALDEMAN: No sir, we don't want you to.

PRESIDENT: You call them in.

HALDEMAN: Good deal.

PRESIDENT: Play it tough. That's the way they play it and that's the way we are going to play it....

PRESIDENT: O.K....Just say (unintelligible) very bad to have this fellow Hunt, ah, he knows too damned much....If it gets out that this is all involved, the Cuba thing, it would be a fiasco. it would make the CIA look bad, it's going to make Hunt look bad, and it is likely to blow the whole Bay of Pigs thing which we think would be very unfortunate--both for CIA, and for the country, at this time, and for American foreign policy. Just tell him to lay off. Don't you [think] so?

HALDEMAN: Yep. That's the basis to do it on. Just leave it at that....

September 15, 1972

PRESIDENT: We are all in it together. This is a war. We take a few shots and it will be over. We will give them a few shots and it will be over. Don't worry. I wouldn't want to be on the other side right now. Would you?

DEAN: Along that line, one of the things I've tried to do, I have begun to keep notes on a lot of people who are emerging as less than our friends because this will be over some day and we shouldn't forget the way some of them have treated us.

PRESIDENT: I want the most comprehensive notes on all those who tried to do us in. They didn't have to do it. If we had had a very close election and they were playing the other side I would understand this. No--they were doing this quite deliberately and they are asking for it and they are going to get it. We have not used the power in this first four years, as you know....We have not used the Bureau, and we have not used the Justice Department, but things are going to change now. And they are either going to do it right or go.

DEAN: What an exciting prospect.

PRESIDENT: Thanks. It has to be done. We have been (adjective deleted) fools for us to come into this election campaign, and not do anything with regard to the Democratic Senators who are running, et cetera. And who the hell are they after? They are after us. It is absolutely ridiculous. It is not going to be that way any more.

GEORGE BUSH ON AGGRESSION IN THE GULF, 1990

The founding of the United Nations embodied our deepest hopes for a peaceful world. And during the past year, we've come closer than ever before to realizing those hopes. We've seen a century sundered by barbed threats and barbed wire, give way to a new era of peace and competition and freedom....

Two months ago, in the waning weeks of one of history's most hopeful summers, the vast, still beauty of the peaceful Kuwaiti desert was fouled by the stench of diesel and the roar of steel tanks. And once again, the sound of distant thunder echoed across a cloudless sky. And once again, the world awoke to face the guns of August.

But this time, the world was ready. The United Nations Security Council's resolute response to Iraq's unprovoked aggression has been without precedent. Since the invasion on August 2, the Council has passed eight major resolutions setting the terms for a solution to the crisis. The Iraqi regime has yet to face the facts. But as I said last month, the annexation of Kuwait will not be permitted to stand. And this is not simply the view of the United States. It is the view of every Kuwaiti, the Arab League, the United Nations. Iraq's leaders should listen. It is Iraq against the world.

Let me take this opportunity to make the policy of my Government clear. The United States supports the use of sanctions to compel Iraq's leaders to withdraw immediately and without condition from Kuwait. We also support the provision of medicine and food for humanitarian purposes, so long as distribution can be properly monitored. Our quarrel is not with the people of Iraq. We do not wish for them to suffer. The world's quarrel is with the dictator who ordered that invasion.

Along with others, we have dispatched military forces to the region to enforce sanctions, to deter and if need be defend against further aggression. And we seek no advantage for ourselves, nor do we seek to maintain our military forces in Saudi Arabia for one day longer than is necessary. U.S. forces were sent at the request of the Saudi Government.

But the world's key task, now, first and always, must be to demonstrate that aggression will not be tolerated or rewarded....

We have a vision of a new partnership of nations that transcends the cold war; a partnership based on consultation, cooperation and collective action, especially through international and regional organizations; a partnership united by principle and the rule of law and supported by an equitable sharing of both cost and commitment; a partnership whose goals are to increase democracy, increase prosperity, increase the peace and reduce arms....

PRESIDENT BILL CLINTON'S REMARKS TO THE CONVOCATION OF
THE CHURCH OF GOD IN CHRIST IN MEMPHIS
November 13, 1993

If Martin Luther King, who said, "Like Moses, I am on the mountaintop, and I can see the promised land, but I'm not going to be able to get there with you, but we will get there," If he were to reappear by my side today and give us a report card on the last 25 years, what would he say? You did a good job, he would say, voting and electing people who formerly were not electable because of the color of their skin. You have more political power, and that is good. You did a good job, he would say, letting people who have the ability to do so live wherever they want to live, go wherever they want to go in this great country. You did a good job, he would say, elevating people of color into the ranks of the United States Armed Forces to the very top or into the very top of our Government. You did a very good job, he would say. He would say, you did a good job creating a black middle class of people who really are doing well, and the middle class is growing more among African-Americans than among non-African-Americans. You did a good job. You did a good job in opening opportunity.

But he would say, I did not live and die to see the American family destroyed. I did not live and die to see 13-year-old boys get automatic weapons and gun down 9-year-olds just for the kick of it. I did not live and die to see young people destroy their own lives with drugs and then build fortunes destroying the lives of others. That is not what I came here to do. I fought for freedom, he would say, but not for the freedom of people to kill each other with reckless abandon, not for the freedom of children to have children and the fathers of the children walk away from them and abandon them as if they don't amount to anything. I fought for people to have the right to work but not to have whole communities and people abandoned. This is not what I lived and died for.

I think finally we may be ready to do something about it. And there is something for each of us to do. There are changes we can make from the outside in, that's the job of the president and the congress and the governors and the mayors and the social service agencies. Then there's some changes we're going to have to make from the inside out, or the others won't matter. That's what that magnificent song was about, wasn't it? Sometimes there are no answers from the outside in; sometimes all the answers have to come from the values and the stirrings and the voices that speak to us from within.

"We were whole." And I say to you, we have to make our people whole again....

So I say to you, we have to make a partnership, all the Government Agencies, all the business folks, but where there are no families, where there

245

is no order, where there is not hope, where we are reducing the size of our armed services because we have won the cold war, who will be there to give structure, discipline, and love to these children? You must do that. And we must help you.

Scripture says, you are the salt of the Earth and the light of the world. That if your light shines before men they will give glory to the Father in heaven. That is what we must do. that is what we must do. How would we explain it to Martin Luther King if he showed up today and said, yes, we won the cold war. Yes, the biggest threat that all of us grew up under, communism and nuclear war, communism gone, nuclear war receding. Yes, we developed all these miraculous technologies. Yes, we all have got a VCR in our home. It's interesting. Yes, we get 50 channels on the cable. Yes, without regard to race, if you work hard and play by the rules, you can get into a service academy or a good college, you'll do just great. How would we explain to him all these kids getting killed and killing each other? How would we justify the things that we permit that no other country in the world would permit? How could we explain that we gave people the freedom to succeed, and we created conditions in which millions abuse that freedom to destroy the things that make life worth living and life itself? We cannot.

And so I say to you today, my fellow Americans, you gave me this job, and we're making progress on the things you hired me to do. But unless we deal with the ravages of crime and drugs and violence and unless we recognize that it's due to the breakdown of the family, the community, and the disappearance of jobs, and unless we say some of this cannot be done by Government, because we have to reach deep inside to the values, the spirit, the soul, and the truth of human nature, none of the other things we seek to do will ever take us where we need to go.

So in this pulpit, on this day, let me ask all of you in your heart to say we will honor the life and the work of Martin Luther King, we will honor the meaning of our church, we will somehow by God's grace, we will turn this around. We will give these children a future. We will take away their guns and give them books. We will take away their despair and give them hope. We will rebuild the families and the neighborhoods and the communities. We won't make all the work that has gone on here benefit just a few. We will do it together by the grace of God.

ATTRIBUTIONS

A Letter of Christopher Columbus, R.H. Major, Select Letters of Christopher Columbus. (London, 1870), pp. 1-17.

Mayflower Compact, F.N. Thorpe (ed.), Federal and State Constitutions. 1909 v. VIII, p. 1841.

William Bradford of Plymouth Plantation, Connecticut Case Studies: The Pequot War. Hartford Steam Boiler Co.

Fundamental Orders of Connecticut, Documents of Connecticut Government. 1994.

Selections From Connecticut's Early Laws, Connecticut Case Studies, Dissenters and the Standing Order. Hartford Steam Boiler Co.

Resolutions of the Stamp Act Congress, Journal of the First Congress of the American Colonies in Opposition to the Tyrannical Acts of the British Parliament, p. 27.

Benjamin Franklin Responds to House of Commons, (1813) XVI 138-159 Passim.

Declaration of Independence

Articles of Confederation

The Northwest Ordinance, F.N. Thorpe, Federal and State Constitutions, v. 11, pp. 957-962

Constitution of the United States

Report on Manufactures-Alexander Hamilton-House of Representatives, December 5, 1791.

Alien and Sedition Acts, U.S. Statutes at Large, v. 1, p. 566.

Marbury v. Madison - 1 Cranch 137 (1'803)

Constitution of Connecticut, Documents of Connecticut Government, 1994.

Missouri Crisis and Impact, A.A. Lipscomb and A.E. Berg, eds., The Writings of Thomas Jefferson, Washington, D.C., 1903 v. 15 p. 247.

James Monroe, Message to Congress, J.D. Richardson, ed., Messages and Papers of the Presidents, vol. 11, p. 407.

Andrew Jackson Endorses Indian Removal, J.D. Richardson, Messages and Papers of the Presidents, vol. 11. p. 207.

Andrew Jackson Vetoes the Bank, J.D. Richardson, Messages and Papers of the Presidents, vol. 11, pp. 456-469.

Seneca Falls Declaration, E.C. Stanton, S.B. Anthony and M.S. Gage, History of Women's Suffrage (New York: Fowler Wells, 1881) v. 1 pp. 70-73.

Dred Scott v. Sandford, 19 Howard (U.S.) 393 (1857).

Slavery in the South, U.S. Government Printing Office, 1957. p. 18, Series 119-134.

Lincoln-Douglas Debates, The Writings of Abraham Lincoln, Constitutional ed. vol. III-IV.

State of Mississippi-Orders of Secession, Laws of Mississippi, 1865. p. 2.

The Gettysburg Address, The Writings of Abraham Lincoln, Constitutional ed. vol. VII, p. 2.

Abraham Lincoln's Second Inaugural Address, Nicolay and Hay, Complete Works of Abraham Lincoln. Lincoln University Memorial ed. n.p. 1894 XI, 44-47.

Black Codes of Louisiana-Louisiana State Statues (1865).

South Must be Punished, Thaddeus Stevens, Reconstruction: Lancaster Examiner Herald. Sept. 7, 1865.

Civil Rights Act, 1875, U.S. Statutes at Large, vol. XXXVII p. 335.

Chinese Exclusion Act, U.S Statues at Large, vol. XXII, p. 58.

Excerpts from Cheap Labor, Bureau of Labor Statistics, State of Connecticut. Nov. 30, 1885.

Populist Party Platform-Edward McPherson, A Handbook of Politics for 1892, (Washington, D.C., 1892), p. 269.

Plessy v. Ferguson, 163 U.S. 537 (1896).

William McKinley's War Message, J.D. Richardson, ed., Messages and Papers of the Presidents, vol. 10, p. 139.

Roosevelt Corollary to the Monroe Doctrine, J.D. Richardson, Messages and Papers of the United States, vol. X pp. 831-832.

Woodrow Wilson's New Freedom, U.S. Senate Document, 63rd Congress, Special Session 1913, vol. I #3, pp. 3-6.

Woodrow Wilson on Neutrality, U.S. Senate Document 566, 63rd Congress, 2nd Session, p. 3-4.

Herbert Hoover on American Values, Campaign Address, October 28, 1928.

Franklin D. Roosevelt Inaugural Address, Pamphlet, U.S. Government Printing Office, Washington, D.C.

Franklin D. Roosevelt's Four Freedoms Speech, U.S. Senate Document, 77th Congress, 2nd Session #188, pp. 81-87.

Franklin D. Roosevelt War Message-Japan, Public Papers of the Presidents of the United States: Franklin D. Roosevelt: 1941, p. 5514.

The Truman Doctrine, Congressional Record, March 12, 1947, pp. 1999-2000.

Truman's Statement on Korea, Senate Foreign Relations Committee Hearing, Military Situation in the Far East, 82nd Congress, 1st Session, p. 3369.

Internal Security Act, 81st Congress, Second Session, Public Law 831.

Sen. Margaret Chase Smith, Congressional Record, 2nd Session, pp. 7894-95, 1950.

Brown v. Board of Education, 347 U.S. 492-495 (1954).

Eisenhower Sends Federal Troops, Presidential Address, Sept. 24, 1957.

Dwight D. Eisenhower's Farewell Address, <u>Public Papers of the Presidents of the United States: Dwight D. Eisenhower</u> (1961), pp. 1035-1040.

John F. Kennedy Inaugural Address, <u>Public Papers of the Presidents of the United States: John F. Kennedy</u>, 1961, pp. 1-3.

John F. Kennedy and the Cuban Missile Crisis, <u>Public Papers of the Presidents of the United States: John F. Kennedy</u>, 1962, pp. 806-809.

John F. Kennedy and the Strategy of Peace, <u>Public Papers of the Presidents of the United States: John F. Kennedy</u>, 1963, pp. 472-479.

Gulf of Tonkin Resolution, <u>Department of State Bulletin</u>, August 29, 1964, p. 268.

Lyndon B. Johnson and the Great Society, <u>Public Papers of the Presidents of the United States: Lyndon B. Johnson</u>, 1965, pp. 394-399.

President Johnson Supports Civil Rights, <u>Public Papers of the Presidents of the United States: Lyndon B. Johnson</u>, 1965, pp. 281-287

President Johnson Asserts His War Aims, <u>Public Papers of the Presidents of the United States: Lyndon B. Johnson</u>, 1966, p. 396.

The Kerner Report, <u>Presidential Commission of Urban Disorders,</u> 1967.

Richard Nixon Sends Troops to Cambodia, <u>Department of State, Bulletin</u>, May 18, 1970.

White House Conversations, U.S. Congress, <u>House of Representatives Report</u> #93-1305, 93rd Congress, 2nd Session, pp. 1-2. 1974.

<u>George Bush on Aggression in the Gulf</u>, United Nations General Assembly, New York, Oct. 1, 1990.

President Bill Clinton's Remarks, President Clinton's Speech, White House Press Office, Nov. 13, 1993.